"Dr. Len Felder possesses uncommon skill in drawing universal wisdom from sacred texts and then applying the fruit of these teachings to modern-day challenges both personal and interpersonal. He guides readers through seven accessible and thought-provoking chapters to boost our energy, open our hearts, overcome fear, and deal more effectively with the pressures of the 24/7 society we live in. 'More Fully Alive' provides clear and practical strategies for navigating life's very narrow bridges."

--Debra Darvick, author of "This Jewish Life" and co-creator of the "Picture a Conversation" discussion card series.

"Who knew that timeless wisdom would turn out to be so timely. Guided by the keen insights of Leonard Felder, we all gain access to a path of life that adds resilience, compassion, and strength, thereby allowing us to live that much better and to shape communities of true caring and belonging. This book is the portal to being more fully alive!"

--Rabbi Bradley Shavit Artson, D.H.L., author of "Passing Life's Tests" and "Renewing the Process of Creation"

"With a wealth of experience and insights, Dr. Felder offers specific methods to achieve a healthier life, grounded in Jewish wisdom. Following his lead, we can begin an inner dialogue, learning how to inquire of ourselves and respond from deep within saying 'To life!'"

--Tamar Frankiel, Ph.D., author of "The Gift of Kabbalah" and "The Voice of Sarah"

"I loved reading this beautiful, practical book on how to create a more mindful life. These 7 accessible chapters are like having a compassionate, skilled companion walk alongside you on the path. I will absolutely recommend it to my students and to my community."

**--Rabbi Jill Berkson Zimmerman,
Founder of The Jewish Mindfulness Network**

"Dr. Felder skillfully weaves the teachings of Jewish tradition and the tools of contemporary psychology into a work that will move readers toward a greater serenity of spirit. First rate!"

--Rabbi Daniel B. Syme, author of "Finding God: 10 Jewish Responses" and "Why I am a Reform Jew"

"In this wonderfully readable book, Dr. Len Felder offers the insights and energy of important Jewish texts in bite size pieces and guides us in using them to help balance our complicated lives. Whether you consider yourself 'religious' or 'not very religious' or 'just spiritual,' his friendly and realistic application of Jewish concepts makes this book a must read for individuals of all backgrounds who wish to live well and to develop the courage to consider new ways to apply profound wisdom."

--Janet Sternfeld Davis, Talmud Teacher and Coordinator of the Beit Midrash, American Jewish University

"Leonard Felder's book 'More Fully Alive' is a great addition to my toolbox for life. I really love the way he uses Jewish wisdom to further my understanding of how to live fully.   His writing style is clear, and his specific examples make it easy to understand how the lessons fit into my life, while deepening my appreciation and connection to my Jewish traditions and philosophies (which can sometimes seem over-intellectual or too dense).   Everyone can benefit from this book on how to deal with your fears, anxieties, and other issues we face in our day-to-day life. I highly recommend it.   Read it and reread it."

--Lisa Loeb, Singer/Songwriter, Parent, and Eyeglasses Designer Grammy-nominated for "Stay (I Missed You)"

MORE FULLY ALIVE

The Benefits of Using Jewish Wisdom for Responding to Stress and Overload

Leonard Felder Ph.D.

author of
The Ten Challenges, Here I Am,
and **When Difficult Relatives Happen to Good People**

JFuture Books
2566 Overland Avenue, #780
Los Angeles CA 90064
www.MoreFullyAlive.net

First Edition
Printed in the United States of America
ISBN 9780692621509
ISBN: 0692621504

Medical Safety: Each individual is unique and if you are currently under the care of a physician or a mental health professional, please continue to follow what you and this trained professional have agreed upon for your health and well-being.   The methods described in this book are not a replacement for the individualized care you are receiving, but rather can be an additional source of support and perspective.

DEDICATION

This book is dedicated to Linda and Steven
for all the growth, laughter, courage and caring
that we share together every day.

CONTENTS

INTRODUCTION

Several years ago I was asked to be on a panel of psychologists discussing how to deal more effectively with stress, anxiety, family tensions, and career difficulties. Since a few of my books have explored Jewish spiritual methods for personal growth and mindfulness (a word that means responding with more consciousness and compassion to challenging situations), the panel facilitator asked me:

"Do you think Jews tend to be anxious?"

I said, "Is the Pope Catholic?"

The Upside and Possible Downside of Angst
Anyone (from any ethnicity or background) can feel anxious or overloaded at times. But those of us who are Jews (whether you are very Jewish, somewhat Jewish, or barely Jewish) tend to have an extra dose of anxiety and pressure that we carry in our nerves and our hearts. (You may have noticed that nearly every Jewish holiday boils down to three things: they tried to kill us, they failed, now let's eat! Or that a Jewish student in high school or college with a report card of all A's and one B is likely to be asked by his or her parent, "So...what's with the B?")

I hope I didn't make you more anxious just now about being both Jewish and anxious. Psychological studies have shown that

a moderate amount of stress and anxiety can be a good thing because it wakes us up pro-actively to challenges we need to deal
with and it motivates us to take action.   It has been shown that
the moderately-anxious person, who can anticipate and deal with
tough situations ahead of time, quite often does much better than
the anxiety-free person who stays too long in a numbing state of
denial.   The person who uses anxious thoughts and feelings as an
early-alert wake-up call to become more creative and resourceful is
going to be far more successful in all sorts of situations where the
spaced-out, clueless, or dismissive individual is at a disadvantage.

Yet these same research studies reveal the important fact that
too much unrelenting stress and worry can become a chronic
drain on our energy, which can jeopardize our health and our
resilience.   Forcing your kishkas (your intestines), your nerve endings, and your lungs to put up with an intense daily dose of worry
and angst day after day, year after year, is likely to cause physical
and emotional symptoms.   Numerous research studies have shown
that chronic stress or a frequent feeling of "I'm drowning and I
can't catch up to what's on my 'To Do' list" or "I'll never be secure
or relaxed" can provoke all sorts of skin problems, muscle aches,
digestive problems, sleep problems, mood swings, as well as some
very serious physical ailments and chronic conditions.

Finding the Right Tools
What can be done to shift the way you (or someone you care about
who is quite anxious) can begin to deal more effectively with the
stress and overload that are a definite part of one's life each day
and each week?   Is there something that can help you feel more
fully alive and less dragged down by all that is on your packed
schedule?

For more than thirty years, I've been counseling good people—
men and women from all walks of life and diverse backgrounds—
who have very busy lives and many conflicting demands on their

time and energy.   They usually come to therapy to deal with a troubled relationship, a frustrating career situation, a painful loss or tragedy, or a desire to reconnect with some aspect of their unique soul that has been held back or pushed aside for too long.

In addition, most people come to therapy to pick up practical and useful clues and insights on how to live each day with more creativity and wisdom, or how to juggle the various responsibilities and demands on your time and energy. My job as a therapist is to explore with each individual client a variety of specific life-enhancing tools that can help him or her respond much better to whatever stresses and tough decisions arise on any given day.   We often can't control the tough situations that pop up in our busy lives, but we can do a much better job of responding to these situations with a much stronger sense of compassion, resilience, and higher perspective.

The book you are about to read is a brief collection of quick and powerfully effective tools that you can utilize immediately in the middle of a rough day or a complicated, demanding moment to make sure you are bringing out your best and not falling back into old habits of impatience, reactivity, or grumpiness.   Rather than you getting twisted up during an important but stressful moment, these accessible tools can help you experience a much greater sense of personal effectiveness and excellent decision-making in situations that formerly knocked you on your butt or caused you to feel frustrated and unsupported.

A Personal Note
Like many people, I didn't know when I was growing up what might be the best methods for dealing with tough situations.   There were a number of challenging moments during my early years that definitely were beyond what I knew how to handle.

For example, I began to realize at a young age that there was a cloud of lingering pain and fear in my family.   My European-born father had barely survived the Holocaust and he lost most of his relatives in the concentration camps. We tried not to bring up the past because we could sense how much pain it caused my hardworking father. But sometimes at the dinner table when I didn't finish all my vegetables, I would be told that I was "letting down the six million who died." Only later did I fully understand the impact of those words—that somehow any slip-up on my part might unintentionally dishonor the millions of souls who had perished during those nightmarish years.

My mother was born in the United States, in a more secure situation, but when I was ten years old she was diagnosed with cancer and she spent the next four years dealing with brutal chemotherapy side-effects, intense mood swings, and progressively declining health until she died when I was fourteen.

My mom was only 46—a highly-intelligent woman who never got the chance to live her dreams. It was so clear at every family gathering from then on that each of her loved ones (especially her parents, her widowed husband, her siblings, and my sister and I) felt devastated to lose her.

Not knowing how to successfully process these and many other painful dilemmas during my early years, I found that I had acquired by the time I reached 23 years old a variety of physical symptoms and internal distress. Since I'm a guy (and guys are not supposed to ask for help or directions, even when they feel a bit lost), I thought I should just keep it all inside and keep plugging away at life. But I realized in my mid-20's that my first long-term relationship was not going well and my first choice of career had turned out to be somewhat of a detour from my deeper calling.

I remember waking up one morning at the age of 24 and wondering, "Is this how it's going to be from now on—a life of inner agitation, painful disappointments, and just going through the motions without much joy or sense of purpose? Or is there another way?"

That was the year when I began to search for and put into practice some of the resilience methods and refocusing techniques that eventually turned my life around. I learned about and tested in real-life situations numerous possible methods before I began to rely on a few extremely effective tools that have worked consistently whenever I remembered to use them immediately in the middle of a tough situation.

I am extremely thankful that I've had the chance to learn from many compassionate and wise women and men on what works and what doesn't work for becoming much healthier and more fully alive even during tough days and stressful weeks. I am still seeking and learning. But every day of my life I am grateful to have found some highly-useful tools for dealing far more effectively with the stresses that still arise in my career, my family responsibilities, several volunteer activities, and being a constantly involved parent of a vulnerable child with special needs whom I love dearly.

Once I realized that these particular, easy-to-learn tools worked consistently in my own life, I began to offer them to some of my counseling clients who expressed an interest in alternative methods for dealing with stress and overload. The seven tools you will learn in the seven chapters of this book have already helped thousands of women and men I have counseled since I became a licensed psychologist in my mid-30's and when I later studied to become a spiritual direction mentor in my mid-40's.

I can't name names, but I can tell you that the creative and smart women and men who were referred to me for counseling sessions and who have tested out these particular methods as a result of our one-on-one confidential conversations included:

- numerous rabbis, cantors, pastoral counselors and adult education teachers from a variety of denominations who wanted to learn more about how to combine psychology and spirituality for dealing with stress and overload.

- spouses and children of clergy who wanted to find creative ways to deal with the pressures of living in a fish bowl.
- many individuals who were moderately or strongly religious or spiritual, and who wanted to learn alternative methods for dealing with tough situations and busy schedules.
- a number of women and men who would not call themselves religious or spiritual, because they had felt alienated from organized religion, but they were still a bit curious about a non-judgmental spiritual approach that wasn't dogmatic or rigid.

Each of these individuals has given me feedback on which tools they found most effective and which methods were easiest to utilize during life's most stressful moments. I appreciate how honest and genuine my diverse counseling clients have been at teaching me which methods work beautifully and which methods need to be discarded from the menu of choices.

What About You and Your Loved Ones?
As you think about your own life and the life of your closest family members and friends, have you ever wondered:

- Is there a better and more satisfying way to deal with the frustrations and time pressures you or a loved one have been experiencing at work, in your family, or in your efforts to make a difference in the world?
- Is there a lingering sense of inner agitation or impatience that eats away at you or a loved one (or that leaks out every so often at people you live with or work with)?
- Is there some fear, sadness, or old habit that is holding you or a loved one back from your fullest potential?

- Is there an unmet longing in your soul for something profound or meaningful that is more fulfilling than the same-old routines you (or certain family members or friends) have been putting up with lately?
- Is there a particular person or a particular situation in your life recently that tends to bring out your indecisiveness, your short fuse, or your inability to follow through on what you know in your heart you wish you could do?

Where These Tools Come From
I had thought in my mid-20's when I went back to graduate school to complete a PhD in Counseling Psychology that the best solutions for stress and anxiety would probably come from my psych professors and from the science of psychology. But instead I have found during the past 35 years of studying with numerous teachers and health practitioners that the most useful and accessible tools for daily resilience and being more fully alive have come from a difference source—from my research into the profound methods of Jewish spirituality which I have tested out in my own life and with many of my counseling clients over these years. I am still a psychologist who loves science, but I am also someone who loves the usefulness and profound wisdom of the stress remedies and healing options that come from Jewish spirituality.

Whether you are Jewish or non-Jewish, quite religious, not-very-religious, or somewhat alienated from religion at the moment, you can test out each of these powerful remedies for yourself in your daily life and see if they work for you (or if they can help someone you care about who is struggling lately with stress or feelings of overload).

What to Expect
In each of the seven short chapters that follow, you will learn in depth about one particular life-enhancing tool per chapter. Not only will you understand where these tools come from and how

they work in daily real-life situations, but you will discover for your-self whether or not they make an impact on the quality of your health, your vitality, and your most important work and personal relationships. For example:

- In Chapter One ("Reconnecting with the Nourishing Breath of Life"), you will discover a deeply spiritual method from ancient Jewish writings for boosting your energy, clarity and creativity during especially stressful moments. It not only improves your breathing and health, but also shifts your perspective and insightfulness to a higher plane.
- In Chapter Two ("Opening Your Heart Even When You're Feeling Impatient"), you will experience a quick and powerful way to expand your compassion, receptivity and responsiveness exactly at the moments when you are starting to shut down, tune out, or harden your heart. Derived from both ancient and modern Jewish teachings, this powerful method for healing inner turmoil will not only benefit your own well-being but will make a significant difference in how you work through the tensions you have with people in your personal life, at work, or in your volunteer activities.
- In Chapter Three ("Finding a Healthy Balance in Situations that Used to Rattle You"), there will be a chance to turn each tough decision, dilemma or competing demand on your time into a breakthrough moment where you find the best possible balance between being either too nice or too tough. Whether you are parenting a child, caring for an aging family member, dealing with intense situations at work, or trying to repair some part of the world, this very accessible Kabbalistic method for balancing compassion and firmness will give you a new level of clarity and mindfulness.
- In Chapter Four ("Addressing the Fears and Pressures that Constrict You"), you will be given the opportunity to

practice a quick meditation technique that is several centuries old but has enormous practicality and inspiration for those who are using it in the 21st century. Based on the mystical teachings of Rabbi Nachman of Bratslav, a Hasidic master in the 18th century, this centering phrase can shift the way you see anxiety-provoking situations and turn a feeling of overwhelm into a renewed sense of resilience and strength.

- In Chapter Five ("Treating Your Body with Greater Understanding and Care"), you will gain practice on how to use Jewish mantras for relaxing your body, recharging your energy, and restoring your body's healing potential even when you are under a lot of pressure or juggling several important responsibilities on the same day.

- In Chapter Six ("Exploring Inner Repair and Outer Repair"), you will find a few moments each day when you will be able to do something quick and mindful that takes important steps to repair either a wound you have inside yourself or a brokenness that you see in the world. Rather than feeling rushed, overloaded or frustrated by the many challenging things you encounter from your Inner Work and Outer Work, you will then be able to feel a sense of slow-but-steady progress. This shift in perspective and effectiveness will come as a result of learning and utilizing a powerful tool from Jewish teachings that are 2,000 years old but extremely relevant today.

- In Chapter Seven ("Enjoying Mini-Sabbaticals Each Day and Each Week"), you will begin to experiment with Jewish methods for letting go for a few minutes each day or for several hours each weekend so that you can see your life, your loved ones, and the world around you with new eyes. There are some amazing breakthroughs that can happen for your health and your aliveness when you try out these ancient and modern practices for transitioning from intense activity to nourishing relief and then back again. Your body, your mind, and your spirit will thank you for learning how to find the right balance of working hard and letting go each day and each week.

CHAPTER 1

RECONNECTING WITH THE

NOURISHING BREATH OF LIFE

Here's a question you probably don't get asked too frequently: Do you consider yourself to be someone who knows how to breathe fully and consciously? Or does your breathing (especially when you are stressed or overloaded) tend to be shallow, constricted, or not very energizing?

I'm not judging, I'm just asking. In fact, I didn't know I was lousy at breathing until a woman with a thick Brooklyn accent told me so. At that time I was living in Manhattan and I felt extremely stressed from a high-pressure job, a strained relationship, and a sense of always rushing and never feeling caught up on the long list of things I felt I needed to do each day.

So I went to see a body-mind therapist on the Upper West Side who specialized in stress reduction methods. After some initial conversation, she abruptly asked me to breathe fully in and out. I had been told by a friend that this therapist was tough, innovative, smart, and humorous. But I still was surprised when she barked at me in her Brooklyn accent, "Are you gonna breathe or are you just gonna sit there?"

I began breathing in and out in a shallow, constricted manner, which wasn't doing very much to reduce the tension in my shoulders, neck, back, and legs. Then she barked at me again:

"Hey Mr. In-Your-Head-All-the-Time, either send some oxygen up and down your body or you're going to die way too soon."

I looked up and saw that despite her barking tone and her thick accent, there was caring and concern in her eyes.

So I took a deep, slow, connected breath that pulled energy up to the top of my skull and filled my abdomen, followed by an exhale that felt like letting go of the high-pressure emotional load I had been carrying. I suddenly felt awake, alert, and more fully alive than usual.

"Do it again, Mr. In-Your-Head-All-the-Time," she barked once more.

I took another deep, slow, connected breath in and out. This time, the clarity and vitality became even stronger. I felt like I'd entered a different way of being.

The Difference Between Lousy and Great Breathing
What I discovered later is that this tough-but-tender therapist was utilizing a profound method that has deep roots in both medical science and Jewish spirituality. There have been many books, articles, and research studies done on how to use breathing methods like this to improve one's health, creativity, responsiveness, and daily effectiveness. I'll describe the science first and then the spiritual aspects.

The Science of What Happens When You Breathe More Fully and Smoothly
Especially in the past few decades, many scientific research studies have explored the health benefits and improved interactions that occur when a person becomes more conscious of breathing in and out in a deep, calm, centered way.

For example, the Framingham study was a 30 year clinical research project involving over 5,000 residents of a small town in Massachusetts that found increased longevity and improved health for individuals who learned how to use breathing and other lifestyle-enhancing methods to overcome stressful situations and hypertensive reactions. A person's breath flow rate and vital capacity were shown to have a big impact on preventing illness or recovering from a variety of stress-related physical symptoms.

More recently at the Cleveland Clinic in Ohio, a team of doctors and researchers led by Mladen Golubic, MD, have been studying what specific daily re-energizing tools and methods can improve various medical symptoms and our emotional well-being. These researchers have included breathing exercises in their lifestyle improvement training program for adults. Hundreds of participants have been studied and it has been demonstrated that these breathing exercises and other stress management tools can dramatically improve a person's inflammatory markers that have been shown to be the source of many acute and chronic diseases. Rather than having to rely on complicated inflammatory-focused medications that sometimes have serious side-effects, these breathing exercises and lifestyle management tools have helped many people prevent various illnesses or recover much quicker from them.

For several years at the National Institute of Mental Health and more recently at the University of Arizona, Esther Sternberg, MD, has been teaching a wide variety of patients how to use slow, deep breathing and other methods to improve their longevity, immune system resilience, mood management, and emotional well-being. Dr. Sternberg has done a series of studies to establish the connection between how your daily life feels and how it manifests either in physical illness or improved well-being.

At the University of California, Los Angeles, Daniel Siegel, MD, has been studying for many years how our body-mind resilience mechanisms can change and improve from using breathing

exercises and mindfulness (a word that Siegel defines as responding in a conscious and caring way rather than reacting in a mind-
less or reflexive way to various real-life situations). He has shown
that by practicing specific breathing or meditation methods over
a period of time, a person can learn how to be less triggered/reac-
tive and instead become more responsive/choiceful during tough
situations. In addition, Siegel's research also has shown how the
neuron activity of the central nervous system and the brain's decision-making centers actually change somewhat from practicing
these nourishing moments of breathing and mindfulness.

Siegel and numerous other researchers worldwide are now
studying this hopeful phenomenon, which they call neuroplasti-
city (the way we can improve our cells, our nerve connection systems, and our immune system responses by various alternative
methods of healing). Their research studies repeatedly confirm
that conscious breathing, mindful focusing, and responding calmly during stressful situations can shift the chemical reactions of
your brain, your hormone releasing mechanisms, your immune
system triggers, and your nerve endings. In the near future, it is
quite possible that millions of women and men can be taught to
improve how they react to stressful situations and how their bodies
can deal more effectively with the health challenges of having such
demanding family responsibilities and workplace pressures.

The Spiritual Aspects of Breathing

There are also some wonderful Jewish writings and teachings
about the deeper significance of what goes on when you take a
loving, slow, full inhale and exhale to shift your energy from stress
and overload into a delicious feeling of inspiration and vitality. For
example, one of my favorite Jewish spiritual explanations of how to
improve your breathing and your health starts with the fact that in
the Hebrew language there is a fascinating word called "mitzrayim (pronounced mitz-RAH-yim)." You might have heard it many

times at Passover Seder meals or at Sabbath services where there are several prayers that say essentially, "Thank you for helping us to get out of mitzrayim, out of Egypt."

But if you study the root of the word "mitzrayim" you'll notice it has the same letters (tzr, tsur) and the same meaning as the word "tsuris" (narrow straits, difficulties, aggravation, constriction). That's why many Jewish scholars, mystics, and teachers translate the word mitzrayim not just as a physical place called Egypt but as a psychological sense of constriction, tightness, feeling trapped or boxed in, or longing to get out of a narrow place.

Which brings us to the Jewish spiritual insights about what happens during a moment of conscious, delicious breathing. On a busy day, when you are rushing, or when you are feeling stressed, anxious or overloaded, you probably aren't breathing fully and your chest and muscles might feel tight. Your brain is probably not seeing the wider perspective of available options and creative possibilities because your anxious thoughts are causing you to lock onto a restrictive feeling of frustration, narrow options, or painful overwhelm.

If at that moment of constriction or mitzrayim, you suddenly remember to take a full, gentle, loving breath in and out (and you repeat the deep, nourishing inhale and exhale a second time or a third time), you will probably feel a sense of liberation, a sense of openness, a sense of renewed strength and clarity. You will be lifting your energy and your awareness out of narrowness and tightness (mitzrayim) and connecting instead with something much greater and more energizing.

Think about it. One moment you are feeling all pent up and anxious. But after a few deep, loving breaths in and out, you usually begin to feel a renewed energy and a renewed connection to something bigger than just the anxious, tense thoughts inside your brain. According to Jewish teachings, when you take a deep breath in and out, you are connecting your individual soul to the pulsing Soul of the Universe. Here is a practical way to experience that expansiveness in your own busy life:

A Jewish Mantra for Connecting Your Breath to the Pulse of the Universe

There is a beautiful line at the end of Psalm 150, which most experts say was written by King David approximately three thousand years ago. As described in several biographies, David was a passionate red-haired harp player, poet, lover, trouble-maker, warrior, king, talented builder and spiritual seeker.

I can't begin to diagnose King David because I've never met him personally and I don't have any case notes from his psychotherapist. But if you read David's Psalms you will notice that this passionate, multi-talented individual had very extreme mood swings. His mood shifts were sometimes more extreme than Florida weather--where intense winds pound the double-pane windows with torrents of rain one minute and then it becomes perfectly sunny and calm a few minutes later.

At the beginning of many of David's Psalms, he describes feeling deeply depressed, isolated, anxious, and frustrated because of the tough things that are going on in his life at that moment. But then after pouring out his anguish in a passionate poem, David switches at some point in most of his Psalms to a feeling of joy and elevated perspective as he begins to connect with the Creative Source of the Universe. The contrast is striking between the pain and anguish at the beginning of many of the Psalms and the feelings of renewed strength and passionate teamwork that are at the end of the Psalms.

The poet, leader, and spiritual seeker David wrote a particularly passionate and inspiring line at the end of Psalm 150 that has to do with the mystery of human breathing. To understand this profound line of poetry, you need to know that the word "breath" in Hebrew is the word "neshamah." You also need to consider that a deep, connected breath re-energizes your inner essence or your soul. The word "soul" in Hebrew is also the same word "neshamah." "Neshamah" is one of those Hebrew words that has a multi-layered meaning and this one word (which simultaneously means breath/soul/essence/life force) makes you stop and think: is it possible that your individual breathing is somehow connected to the much wider breathing, pulsing, energizing vitality of the universal force field that is flowing constantly around us and inside of us?

Now here's how this expansive idea (a connection between your individual breathing and the breathing of the universe) can be used as a Jewish mantra for reducing stress and raising up your energy: In the final culminating verse of Psalm 150 (which is read or sung in a very lively fashion in many congregations around the world daily, weekly, and yearly), David is feeling especially joyful and alive as he says, "Kol ha-neshamah, t'hallel Yah," which different people translate in different ways as "Everything that has breath is praising the ultimate Source of Life," or "Every soul is praising the infinite Creative Source," or "Every breath is praising the One that is beyond human concepts."

Here is what the words mean--one word at a time:

Kol every, all, everything

Ha-neshamah breath, soul, essence, having breath, having a soul, having an essence

T'hallel praises, honors, acclaims, appreciates, celebrates

Yah the Eternal One, the Source of Life, God, the Ever-Flowing Ongoing Creation

When you say these uplifting words from Psalm 150, you can choose any combination of these translations. You might select the translation you were taught in your own congregation or your religious school education so you can stay true to what is most familiar to you.   Or you might also choose to experiment with a different translation that grabs your heart or boosts your energy in a new way. My personal favorite (though it changes sometimes) is to say:

"Kol Ha-neshamah T'hallel Yah

Every breath celebrates the Source of Life"

I find that particular translation to be the one that stirs up for me (and many people I have counseled) the strongest sense of wonder, curiosity, appreciation, and connection to a wider perspective. Almost every time I take a deep breath in and out while saying "Every breath celebrates the Source of Life," it helps me get out of stress or constriction while opening up the possibility of seeing a tough situation in a new, more creative light.

How It Works in Your Daily Life

What if on a busy day you said silently that energizing phrase at the exact moment you were taking a deep breath in and out? What if you could transform a moment of stress, anxiety or overload into a profound connection between your personal stress-relieving-breath and how that moment of inhaling and exhaling aligns you with the intuitively-felt Creative Flow of the Universe, or the hard-to-describe Source of Life? What if you were no longer trapped in the narrow, anxious, constricting limits of the stressed human brain that you carry on your weary shoulders, but rather you were able to gain access to a continuous and expansive flow of energy and insight that is only a loving breath away.

Please note: I need to pause for a moment to see if any readers have fallen off the tour bus. When I start using phrases like "Creative Flow of the Universe," "Source of Life," or "Infinite One," it's quite possible that you or someone you give this book to will say, "Uh-oh, it's starting to sound a little woo-woo around here."

In Judaism, it is perfectly ok to cringe or be skeptical about imperfect words that attempt to describe the indescribable. If you or a loved one are unsure of whether there is an infinite creative force that is beyond our human understanding, don't worry. Most Jewish scholars, rabbis, and teachers will tell you that it's completely permissible to wrestle with these ideas and concepts. In fact, the word "Yisra-El, Israel," literally means "the person who wrestles and strives with the One-That-Is-Beyond-Human-Words."

In other words, your questions and doubts are perfectly appropriate. In case you haven't noticed already, Jews tend to ask a lot of questions. (If you've ever been to a lively participatory Passover Seder or a creative Torah discussion group, they are definitely about asking deep and important questions).

I remember several years ago when I was touring fifteen Red States and Blue States for my earlier book "The Ten Challenges" (about how to make an ancient text come alive with modern relevance and a diversity of rabbinic interpretations). During each speech at numerous synagogues, churches, libraries, bookstores, and colleges, a surprisingly large number of non-Jews from fundamentalist families would come up to me nervously and ask in a quiet, cautious voice, "Do Jews really have permission to ask such probing questions of their rabbis and wrestle with the ancient words to come up with so many different interpretations?" I said, "Yes, that's what we do."

Many of these audience members would ask again, "Are you sure it's permitted to question what was taught to you by your parents and leaders about the Scriptures?" I replied, "It's not only permitted, it's encouraged to bring up your concerns and different ideas so that each year we can go deeper into what it means and how it applies to our daily lives."

I feel sad that there are so many good people from a variety of backgrounds who have been turned off to religion and spirituality because the big questions of life were presented to them in a harsh "take-it-or-leave-it" manner, or who were not encouraged to express their concerns and explore deeper ways of understanding the mysteries that each generation wrestles with in new ways.

So please don't worry if at times you have doubted or wanted to question what an in-your-face dogmatic person has tried to shove down your throat about the holy energies that are beyond human understanding. For instance, you are not alone if you have ever felt skeptical of a white haired grandpa-like deity up in heaven throwing lightning bolts or some other patriarchal image of a King or Ruler as envisioned by various Renaissance painters. Most Jews (including most rabbis, scholars and regular folks as well) have always been strong and outspoken about not creating a limiting picture or a human-like gender for the Creative Presence that in Judaism is most often called "Ha-Shem, the Name that is far beyond what we limited humans can put in words." Or sometimes this holy mystery is called "Shechinah," which means the in-dwelling Presence, or the expression of the Divine energies that are flowing closest to us.

One of my favorite teachers on this topic, a Jewish meditation instructor I first met over 25 years ago at an awe-inspiring weekend retreat, is Rabbi David Cooper of Boulder, Colorado. He later wrote a book you might have heard about called "God is a Verb" in which Rabbi Cooper explores how a large number of Jewish beliefs and teachings point toward an ever-growing and ever-changing idea of God not as a noun (a noun would be an "it" or a finite "thing"), but rather to explore the possibility of God as a verb (an ever-flowing creative process or continuous energy that changes as we change and is never a static "thing").

Even the great teacher and prophet Moses wrestled with this issue of a God that is beyond human definition and came up with a similar sense of an ever-evolving creative force in the universe. In the Book of Exodus, Chapter 3, verse 14, Moses asks, "If the people of Israel want to know Your Name, what shall I tell them?" According to the original text, the reply that Moses hears is "Ehyeh Asher Ehyeh," which means "I am becoming what I am becoming."

Sounds more like an ongoing, continually expressing process rather than a fixed or static "it."

In Jewish spirituality there is a lot of room to wrestle, change, explore and disagree about what it means to connect with the Eternal One or the One that is Beyond All Human Words. So throughout this book please feel free to question, reject, or offer your own insights and beliefs into what you envision as the endless Breath of Life (another name for God) that I am suggesting can be liberating and life-enhancing if we open up to this universal pulsing energy with our own personal, deep, loving breath in and out. Especially during moments of anxiety, tension, constriction and mitzrayim (narrow straits), your individual soul can be re-energized and expanded by affirming your connection to the unlimited creative Source that flows more smoothly through you with each full breath you take.

Choosing to Breathe More Consciously and More Passionately
Now let's combine the medical science (which has shown repeatedly that fuller breathing is good for your health) and the Jewish spiritual process of aligning your sometimes tense, constricted self with the ever-flowing Breath of Life that surrounds you always (and flows through you if you breathe it in fully and lovingly).

Whenever you are feeling stressed or overloaded, take a moment to envision or say these words ("Kol ha-neshamah, t'hallel Yah, Every breath is celebrating the Source of Life") as you breathe gently, calmly, expansively in and out. You can say the words in Hebrew or in English, or both. You can say it silently with your lips barely moving, or simply hear it silently in your mind where no one will know you are reciting a Jewish mantra.

When your breathing (once, twice, or three times) is aligned for a few seconds with the larger flow of the universe, you will probably feel re-energized and somewhat more aware and open to good ideas. You will be letting yourself be part of the much more expansive Breath of Life, which is possibly the same Universal Flow that causes the birds to know their migratory routes and this Infinite Flow also influences the diverse ways that caring people reach out to those in need and take part daily in the ongoing creation and repair of the world we inhabit.

It doesn't matter if you choose to breathe either nose-in nose-out, or if you feel more comfortable breathing nose-in mouth-out, or if you tend to breathe mouth-in mouth-out. I've seen excellent results occur for people who did any or all of these options for breathing calmly, lovingly, and fully. What matters most is your kavanah (the Hebrew word for "deeper intention") and that you take a moment to say yes to the opportunity to lift up your awareness out of the anxious ruts of the human brain and make sure you align your breathing with a flow of energy, creativity and support that re-awakens your deeper awareness.

A Quick Here-and-Now Experience

How about if you try this breathing and re-energizing method right where you are at this exact moment in time? Just breathe in and out a few times deeply, calmly and lovingly while saying or thinking the ancient words "Kol ha-neshamah t'hallel Yah. Every breath celebrates the Source of Life" in order to find out what these words mean to you personally at this moment. It won't cost you anything and it might gain you a quick sense of freedom from the tensions of the moment. Please stop reading for a few seconds and test it out right now.

After a few connecting breaths in and out, ask yourself:

- Did you breathe a little fuller, calmer, and more lovingly than usual?
- What did it feel like in your stomach, chest, arms and legs to breathe more consciously right in the middle of a busy day?

- Did you experience an increase in your alertness or your energy?
- What did the words "Every breath celebrates the Source of Life" mean to you today as you breathed them into your body, mind and spirit?

Please honor whatever you experienced during this quick experiment and don't judge it as good or bad. Maybe you barely breathed and the words didn't mean much this time. Or maybe you caught a tiny glimpse of what it might feel like to let more oxygen and spiritual expansiveness be a part of your busy life. Or maybe you felt something shift inside you as you opened up to some nourishing breathing and the chance to remember the generous Source of Life that flows through you more fully whenever you allow it.

What If You Don't Want to Breathe More Fully?
Quite often I hear from men and women in therapy sessions and at workshops who tell me they felt various types of resistance, distractibility and impatience when they were asked to breathe in and out more lovingly and consciously. Here are a few of the things I've heard from actual people:

- Concern #1: "I don't have time to breathe or 'get spiritual' in the middle of a busy day. I don't want to become so relaxed that I'll turn into a slacker or get lazy."

    Possible Solution: This common feeling of "I need to stay frenetic or I'll become a slacker" is a myth that you can quickly disprove in less than five seconds when you take a few deep breaths in and out while opening up to a more expansive viewpoint. You won't have wasted any time or "become lazy." Rather, this five second boost of spiritual insight and increased energy will help your brain to consider more possibilities for being more creative and effective with whatever challenges you are facing at this moment.

- Concern #2: "I loved learning about these Jewish methods, but I can't seem to remember to do them during an actual stressful moment."

    Possible Solution: We all tend to forget at times to use helpful tools or remember our soul's essence. But many of my counseling clients have remedied this problem by putting a tiny note card on the back side of their cell phone that says, "Remember to breathe and celebrate the Source of Life" or just "Breathe!" Since most people are constantly reaching for their cell phones, this quick reminder gives you several chances a day to breathe in and out slowly while you say the ancient words of appreciation for the One that flows through us continually.

- Concern #3: "I do remember to breathe sometimes and say the uplifting words to myself. But my brain quickly goes back to worry and stress."

    We all have noisy brains that tend to shift back to anxiety, worry, and problems. But we also have the ability to override this default mechanism in the brain by inserting several times a day a few deep breaths and some uplifting spiritual words such as "Every breath connects me to the ever-flowing Source of Life." Whenever you forget to breathe or you are starting to tense up, use that moment of noticing your own tightness as a chance to shift the energy once again. Without judging yourself or criticizing yourself, simply take another loving breath in and out as you connect with the expansive possibilities one more time. Essentially, you are retraining your brain one day at a time to reconnect with what is uplifting and positive, rather than staying stuck in the narrow anxious thoughts that used to seem irreversible.

- Concern #4: "I guess I'm afraid of asking for too much or trusting that there's a God that cares about me personally."

Many people have a belief that if they ask for too much, if they raise their hopes, or if they stand too tall they will be thwacked down. For example, one of my counseling clients is a woman who learned in her family that if she stood up for herself or prayed for things she cared about, she would be accused of being selfish and un-caring. But in fact this woman was an extremely caring and mostly humble person. She made some progress in her breathing and her daily re-energizing when she changed the words slightly to say, "Kol ha-neshamah t'hallel Yah, Every soul is doing his or her small part of helping the ongoing creation and repair of the world." Instead of being self-conscious about whether she was asking too much or waiting for a sign that God must first respond to her personally, she began to experience a new sense of being part of a much larger chorus of caring souls who were all celebrating together the fact that each one of us is doing our part to fulfill the work of the One that is creating the world continually.

You might need to use several attempts at breathing in and out, or several ways of saying specific word variations that mean more to you personally. But eventually I have found that even the most skeptical or anxious individuals are able to connect their own expanded breathing to the wider Breath of Life that infuses the world constantly with energy and strength. Please don't give up after one or two attempts and please don't worry if your brain (like everyone else's brain) to some extent continues to doubt or question everything we say or do. Brains are quite good at being skeptical and questioning—that is a blessing in many situations when an inquisitive mind helps you sort out validity from nonsense. But you can still breathe and expand your connection to the indefinable Breath of Life even with a partially-skeptical or somewhat-noisy brain.

When Are the Most Beneficial Moments to Breathe and Connect?
It's probably not possible to be a conscious breather 24 hours a day. After all, we are human and our brains spend a lot of time getting distracted and then sometimes remembering to re-connect with what truly matters.

But in spite of our human limitations, there are several times each day when this simple-to-utilize breathing and re-energizing method can help enormously. See if you can breathe a little more and say the ancient words of celebrating your connection to the Source of Life at any or all of the following moments:

- When you are feeling tense or frustrated because someone is getting on your nerves.
- When you are trying to get somewhere and you are being delayed by traffic or someone who is going extra slowly.
- When you are hoping for something and you're anxious that it might not happen.
- When you are recovering from a disappointment, a loss, or a setback.
- When there is something beautiful or inspiring nearby, but your thoughts are somewhere else.
- When something goes right or feels meaningful and you want to embrace this moment before it slips away.
- When you are juggling two things at the same time or feeling caught between the demands of your family and your work.
- When you are working on a creative project or problem-solving on something complicated and you want to make

sure you see the bigger perspective rather than being stuck on one of the irritating details.

- When you are feeling alone or isolated or cut off from what truly matters and you want to reconnect with the bigger picture.
- When during a stressful day you look at someone you care about, or you are on the phone with this person, and you want to breathe, center, and be fully present rather than missing out on this chance to be your best self with this cherished person.

Each of these moments is a chance to break out of constriction, stress and tension so that you can experience a fuller dose of aliveness and creativity. Here are two quick examples of people who benefited from this method of boosting your energy and clarity in the middle of a stressful moment:

- Robert (not his real name) is a very-talented rabbi who came to me for counseling a few months ago because of the tensions and stresses in his over-packed daily schedule and the fact that his marriage seems close to the edge recently. On a typical day, Robert handles at least one irate congregant, several pushy board members, the demands of his two teenage children, the pressures to write sermons that have to be amazing if he wants his contract renewed in two years, plus the arguing between a bat mitzvah student he is advising and the student's divorced parents who are in a power struggle over the details of the upcoming event. In addition, Robert gets a surprise phone call every few weeks telling him that he needs to put his life on hold for a funeral and several days of helping the grieving family.

Like most of us (only more so), he is stressed and overloaded by the non-stop intensity of juggling his personal life and his work responsibilities. He let me know that what he wanted from counseling was not to be told something superficial such as "lighten up" or "take a break" or "bring home flowers." Just like many other quality individuals in the clergy and the helping professions, Robert was looking for a reliable and highly-effective way to stay healthy, strong, and fully-present for each of the vulnerable individuals and cherished loved ones he encounters on a daily basis.

So we began to explore what has been causing him lately to become tense or impatient more than usual with his family and a few "entitled" board members. We also discussed ways to strengthen his relationship and deal more effectively with his two teenagers.

In addition, I asked Robert if he would be willing to experiment for a few seconds several times a day using three deep, calm, energizing breaths while saying "Kol ha-neshamah t'hallel Yah, Every soul is celebrating the Source of Life." At first Robert was reluctant, saying, "I just can't imagine finding even a few seconds to breathe as a result of my busy schedule."

But then on an especially stressful day, he noticed for a moment how tense he was and he quickly breathed in and out calmly and lovingly three times while saying, "Every breath celebrates the Source of Life." Robert told me a few days later, "Wow, it made a huge difference. My brain got clear and focused again. My energy was strong again. I had been feeling burned out and exhausted, but after just three of these deep calm breaths I felt like I'd been given a gift of an extra boost of being able to deal with all that was on my schedule that day."

Robert then began breathing more fully a few times a day while saying the ancient words silently and he discovered, "It really doesn't take much time at all--maybe five seconds or ten seconds maximum. I wish they'd taught me something like this in rabbinic school. Yes, we learned how to race through the prayers and how to understand lots of heady texts. But there is something so pure and transformative about taking a few deep breaths in and out while saying King

David's passionate words of appreciation and praise for the amazing fact of being alive. In just a few quick seconds, I can feel my soul unhooking from most of the pressure and suddenly re-connecting with a loving Presence that replenishes me."

- Sharon (also not her real name) is a highly-intelligent woman with an especially stressful life and some recent health challenges. Even though she was born Jewish, Sharon describes herself as extremely secular and she rarely sets foot in a synagogue or temple. She told me in one of her first counseling sessions, "I'm just not someone who can believe in anything. So please don't judge me for being who I am."

What I found in our counseling sessions is that Sharon, like many people who are uncomfortable with anything dogmatic or rigid, has a quite beautiful sense of calm and transcendence when she is involved in her beloved hobby of gardening.

When I asked Sharon what gardening felt like to her, she explained, "I feel a sense of timelessness and peacefulness when I'm watering, weeding, re-potting, or just enjoying the plants in my small garden."

One day during a counseling session about her favorite ways of rising above the tensions of her busy life, I asked Sharon, "Do you ever feel when you are watering and tending to your plants that you are part of some bigger picture of caring for these fragile and thriving life-forms? Do you ever feel 'called' in some mysterious way to be doing what you do to help nourish and sustain these plants?"

Sharon's eyes began to fill with tears as she admitted, "Yeah, it's hard to describe, but in those moments when I am out in the garden totally focused on each bud, each root, each mound of moistened earth, I seem to be part of an energy or a life force that is beyond words."

What Sharon described as an "energy or a life force that is beyond words" is quite similar to the sense of "neshamah" or "breathing/soul/life force" that connects our individual breath to a pulsing breath of life that is beyond our narrow selves. I would never ask Sharon to call that pleasurable sense of connected breath anything other than what she was comfortable calling it. But during several months in which Sharon began to utilize the breathing method of three deep inhales and exhales several times a day, along with the words, "Every breath celebrates the nourishing life force," she gradually became a lot less stressed and much healthier.

As I said to Sharon (and to many other counseling clients), "I will not judge you or criticize you for whatever words you choose to call the life force, or the flow of loving energy between you and the vulnerable plants. I'm just happy to see you so alive when you're breathing more fully and enjoying your connection to these colorful and delicate life forms."

Enough about clients...now let's consider your own busy schedule: Whether you call the invisible flow of energy by referring to the word "God" or "Ha-Shem (the name)" or "Source of Life" or "creative flow," I hope you find a way to connect with that nourishing energy quickly and often, especially on your busiest days. I also hope that someday all of us humans can stop fighting one another over the names we pick to describe the indescribable. We all have access to that nourishing Source of Life if we take a moment to breathe it deeply into our lungs, our bodies, and our souls. All I ask is that you take a few seconds several times a day to let the endless stream of energy recharge your batteries—and that you use this nourishing energy for healing and repair rather than for harm or insensitivity.

CHAPTER 2

OPENING YOUR HEART

Even When You're Feeling Impatient

Let's be honest. Do you ever have moments when you are in a hurry (or your mind is racing with things to do) and you unintentionally snap with impatience at someone you love? Do you ever find yourself only half-listening when someone in your family or your workplace is needing your full attention about something he or she passionately wants you to hear and understand? Do you ever feel as if you give a lot to so many people that you have nothing more to give?

If so, welcome to the human dilemma. Even if a person deeply desires to be more fully present and compassionate, we all have moments when our hearts are not truly open or when we're not 100% available in a sufficient way for those who need us the most. It's important that we admit to ourselves that staying open and compassionate is not always easy, so we can make some progress on this important aspect of being more fully alive.

This challenging part of being more mindful and effective in relationships (with a roommate, at work, with family, or with a romantic partner) is something that even the most decent and high-integrity people struggle with every so often. For example, I have an extremely caring and thoughtful therapy client named Gayle who mentioned during her initial counseling session that she had recently put a bumper sticker on her car that says, "I Want to Be the Person My Dog Thinks I Am."

Gayle then explained, "With my beloved pet animal, my heart's completely open. My patience and understanding with my adorable dog are far greater than they are with my husband, my mom, my kids, or the people I work with. I can be so loving and wonderfully playful with my dog, but sometimes when my family or my colleagues at work ask for things from me or just want my time and attention on a day when I've overloaded, much too often I notice myself tensing up or cutting them off with an impatient response."

Bear in mind that Gayle is one of the most considerate and decent human beings you will ever meet. But even the most compassionate individuals sometimes realize that there is important additional progress to be made in order to stop snapping at or unintentionally hurting loved ones and co-workers.

When Gayle was courageous enough to admit, "Yes, I sometimes have no patience left and my loved ones and a few of my colleagues have seen the side of me I wish I didn't have," it was the beginning of an enormously useful therapy session in which we began to discover what tends to trigger that impatience and reactivity. Like many compassionate people, Gayle had felt pressured to be "all things to all people" in her family of origin, in her previous marriage, and in dealing with her demanding boss and clients at work. As you might identify with from your own life, Gayle felt a strong desire "not to let anyone down" and so she sometimes did more than was humanly possible and got burned out or exhausted, which often caused her to have "nothing left but a short fuse and a sense of regret."

In our therapy sessions, Gayle explored in detail what it felt like to be overloaded at times by how much others relied on her. She admitted at one point, "I try to be an open and caring person, but the truth is I sometimes notice that in certain situations I tend to be very short-fused, especially with the vulnerable people I care about the most and who need me the most."

Sorting out the past was somewhat helpful, but now what? What could Gayle do to break the cycle of doing too much, getting worn down, and then becoming impatient or short-fused with people she didn't want to hurt or alienate? That is the key question that comes up with many therapy clients (and that I've faced in my own life) and that requires a wonderful tool from Jewish spirituality that can be extremely effective and empowering.

So I asked Gayle, "What if we could find you a little more energy and patience to be that loving, creative person more often, even on busy high-intensity days—with the kind of relaxed openness and caring like you are with your four-legged soul mate?"

Gayle was silent for a moment. Then she said with some sadness in her voice, "I am a bit skeptical…I've had this habit for a long time of doing too much, getting worn out, and then becoming a bit short-fused. To be honest, I just don't see a huge change happening for me. I have spent years trying to be less tense and more open with the people I live with and work with. But it's not easy, especially these past few months with so many challenging things happening in my life."

The Subtle Signs that Your Heart Might Have Become a Bit Hardened

What Gayle and many other good people have discovered is that they deeply desire to live with an open, generous, enduring heart, but every so often they find themselves with a somewhat hardened heart or a quick flash of anger, sarcasm, or impatience. Sometimes we unintentionally say or do things that hurt the people we love or work with because our inner agitation overrides our desire to be caring and receptive to those who mean the most to us.

For a quick moment, consider whether the following indications of a "somewhat hardened heart" sound at all like you or someone you live with or work with:

- Do you sometimes find yourself feeling impatient, closed off, or emotionally burned-out in the middle of a conversation with an aging parent, a vulnerable child, a somewhat-disorganized spouse or roommate, or someone long-winded at work?

- Do you ever notice that your brain is churning with critical or judgmental thoughts about some individual in your personal life or in your workplace who longs for your support and your understanding but who is wanting your complete attention at a moment when you are not genuinely open or receptive?

- Do you ever experience a sense of "compassion fatigue," in which you feel irritated or resentful that a needy person you see on the street, or someone raising money on the phone, or a friend or loved one in a tough situation is asking you for something and you start to feel, "What about me? What about the struggles I have to face?"

- Do you ever wonder if there is some major or minor scar tissue around your heart that it is preventing you from being sufficiently open to love, to creativity, or to living more fully?

- Are you sometimes a bit rough on yourself? Do you ever feel impatient or painfully self-critical regarding your own personal idiosyncrasies or your unconventional way of doing things?

Please don't be horrified if you said "Yes" to one or more of the above questions. My goal is not to depress you or judge you, but rather to empower you to begin the process of reclaiming your own full aliveness. In truth, nearly every human being has short or long periods of time in which we feel somewhat overloaded, edgy, or painfully cut off from our fullest vitality. Admitting to yourself that your heart has been starting to harden with guardedness, impatience, or frustration is a first step toward healing and resilience. Rather than pretending "I never get flustered or closed-off," sometimes there is a huge benefit if we just tell the truth to at least one good listener who can help us honor the fact that we are feeling overloaded or somewhat-agitated lately.

How Do You Re-Open a Partially-Closed Heart?

If you (or someone you know) have recurring moments when your patience seems to be gone or your heart is not fully open, there is something quick, powerful, and effective you can do. The best quick remedy for re-opening your heart and becoming more fully alive again is an extremely practical method that comes from a deeply spiritual series of phrases in the Hebrew Scriptures.

The precise phrase I would like you to consider as a highly-effective tool during tough moments of impatience or frustration comes from the ancient words that were spoken by Moses in the Book of Deuteronomy, as well as being articulated later by the psalmist David, plus being spoken by the prophet Ezekiel, and also by the prophet Jeremiah.

This powerful suggestion of what to do when you are feeling edgy, judgmental, sarcastic, or emotionally closed-off says mysteriously, "Circumcise your heart."

Your first reaction might be, "What? You want me to consider circumcising my delicate heart? Right at the moment when I am feeling threatened or in need of protection? Are you kidding?"

Relax...it will start to make more sense very soon. Take a few seconds and ask yourself, "What do you imagine it means for a human being in the middle of a tense interaction to 'circumcise one's heart?'"

- Does it mean making an actual incision or causing your heart physical harm? The answer is "No," it doesn't require anything surgical, bloody, or dangerous.
- Does it mean punishing yourself or feeling inadequate because you (like every other human being) gets twisted up sometimes and your heart isn't fully open or receptive? The answer is "No," you are not a bad or defective person for sometimes finding yourself with a partially-closed heart.
- Does it mean quickly saying something to yourself that can dependably re-open your heart and re-awaken a deeper level of compassion and responsiveness? The answer is "Yes." To circumcise your heart means to quickly catch yourself starting to shut down and instead set your intention (and most importantly your follow-through) to be more open, loving, and fully present—even during a stressful moment of an over-packed day.
- Does "circumcise your heart" mean turning a painful setback or a frustrating moment into a crucial opportunity to listen, grow, learn and expand beyond what you could do previously? The answer is "Yes," because in Jewish spirituality the painful moment of feeling hurt or upset by someone or something is also the most opportune moment for opening up and becoming more fully alive and compassionate than you've ever been before. It often takes a somewhat broken or shattered heart before we are ready to open up courageously and go beyond our previous defensive postures.

Why Even the Smallest Opening Can Make a Huge Difference
I have found with many counseling clients and in my own personal life that a successful moment of "circumcising your heart" does not require the complete removal of each of the layers of protective covering that most of us has put over our delicate hearts. We are

talking instead about a new tiny sliver of an opening that allows your caring, your patience, and your life force to get unblocked and flowing once again.

As Rabbi Miriam Hamrell, a wonderful teacher and synagogue leader in West Los Angeles has said often in her sermons, writings, and Musar (character development) classes that I've enjoyed each week for the past ten years: "In a completely darkened room, all it takes is the tiniest opening as small as the eye of the needle in order to let in a substantial burst of light. Just a tiny opening can transform an entire room and fill it with light. And all it takes is a tiny opening in your hardened heart that allows your enormous caring and kindness to pour out once again. Just one small opening in the heart can make a huge difference."

In Jewish spiritual teachings, we all have moments when we discover that the protective coverings we have put around our hearts start to block our fullest expression of creativity, love, connection and wisdom. One of the most important things you can do for healing and aliveness is to remove these coverings just enough so that your energy can flow more fully again.

Here are just a few examples of how "opening your heart" or "circumcising your heart" is described in sacred Jewish writings. See which ones speak to you personally as you think about your own impatience or guardedness, and your desire to be more open and compassionate more of the time:

- In Deuteronomy 10:16 it says the way to be more alive and connected is to "circumcise your own heart."
- In Deuteronomy 30:6 it suggests that opening up to the Infinite One that is beyond human comprehension will circumcise your heart and the hearts of your descendants.
- In Jeremiah 4:4 it recommends, "Remove the foreskins of your heart."

- In Ezekiel 36:26 it details, "A new heart also will I give you, and I will take away the stony heart out of your flesh, and give you a more supple fleshy heart."
- In Proverbs 4:23, it explains, "Take care of your heart with vigilance, for from it flows the spring of life."
- In Psalm 34:18 it suggests, "The Eternal One is nearest to those with a broken heart."
- In Psalm 51:17, it says, "God does not delight in sacrifices or burnt offerings, but rather in a broken spirit, a broken and contrite heart."

In other words, when you feel hurt, criticized, wronged, or impatient, that is an especially ripe moment for honoring your temporary brokenness and letting more caring and insight flow through a new tiny opening in your somewhat-hardened heart. But how do you do this successfully, especially when you're feeling agitated or defensive toward someone who has gotten on your nerves recently?

The Quick Inner Shift
What I've experienced thousands of times in my own life and with a wide variety of counseling clients is that during a moment of tension, disagreement or hardening of the heart, all it takes is to say quickly to oneself, "Is my heart open right now?"

Just that one silently-spoken question, "Is my heart open right now," can instantly lift you up out of defensiveness and instead open your heart and your aliveness. Even if you were feeling upset, angry, or agitated a few seconds earlier, the gentle truth-seeking question of "Is my heart open right now" can take you immediately to a more curious, open, and receptive frame of mind.

The only way to find out if it will work for you during tough moments is to try it out a few times. Here are several situations when you might notice your heart is hardening, your impatience is building, and you're not really listening from a compassionate place to the person you are starting to snap at or disregard:

- The next time after a stressful day when you arrive home or sit down for a "How's it going" conversation with someone who needs your love but often receives your impatience, ask yourself, "Is my heart open right now?"
- In the middle of an argument or a battle for control with someone in your personal life or your work life, stop for a moment and silently ask yourself, "Is my heart open right now?"
- When you're feeling tired, physically uncomfortable, or emotionally frustrated and you tend to have a shorter fuse than usual, you can prevent a lot of tension and hurt feelings by saying silently to yourself once or twice, "Is my heart open right now?"
- When you are so sure of your particular point of view and you aren't really considering the possibility that someone else's point of view might also have some truth in it, this would be a good moment to open up your mind and your curiosity with the gentle question, "Is my heart open right now?"
- When you are in nature, or in a spiritual or religious gathering, or when you are in a hospital or nursing home, or at an important school or parent meeting and you get distracted from the precious moment with some anxious or unpleasant thoughts, ask yourself calmly, "Is my heart open right now?"
- When you are replying to someone's email, text, phone call, or tweet and you are tempted to be snarky or negative, ask yourself, "Is my heart open right now" and see what other possibilities there are for responding with greater wisdom, compassion, and the desire to do something positive and healing.

The Dutch Shoe and the Moment of Decision

Asking yourself the question, "Is my heart open right now" can be done very quickly and silently. Quite often you will only have a brief second for deciding whether to snap at someone or to catch yourself and choose instead to open up your heart and listen to this person's differing perspective by asking yourself if your heart is truly open or not at this precise moment.

For example, I remember several years ago when my son Steven, who has special needs, was ten years old and my wife Linda and I took him to Michigan one summer to visit his cousin. On a sunny day, we took Steven a couple hours west to the tourist town of Holland, Michigan where he saw up close a costumed Dutch dancer wearing traditional wooden shoes and making high leg kicks in front of an old windmill.

Steven was fascinated by the colorfully-dressed Dutch dancer and the wooden shoes. So we purchased a hand-carved pair of Dutch shoes for him to bring home to Los Angeles.

A few weeks later I was in the kitchen washing dishes and rushing so that I could get to an appointment on time. Suddenly, I heard a loud crash from Steven's room down the hall.

My heart was beating rapidly and my mind was racing with thoughts like, "I can't deal with this now. What the blank is going on?"

When I reached Steven's room, I saw him with one wooden shoe still on his left foot but his right wooden shoe had flown through the bedroom window and shattered the glass into sharp pieces.

My first reaction (that I did not act upon) was a desire to scream at him or grab him by the shoulders and say, "What did you do here!!!!!" Probably because I grew up with a father who believed in hitting and yelling (since his own father had taught him that this was the way to raise a cooperative child), I sometimes find at a tense moment with my very impulsive son that I can feel the nerves and muscles in my body pulsing and ready to burst forth with an angry quick reaction.

But during that half-second of seeing the shattered window and the worried look on Steven's face, I knew I had to make an important decision. So I tried out the Jewish spiritual method of asking myself, "Is my heart open right now?"

My blood pressure and my adrenal glands were still pumping rapidly. My thoughts were still noisy and racing. But that simple question, "Is my heart open right now," had allowed me to make a quick shift to a more open sense of "What are my options here?"

I took a gentle breath in and out. I felt my heart opening just a little bit more as I stopped myself from the multi-generational urge to shout or grab my son by the shoulders.

Then I took one more soothing breath in and out as I asked my beloved son in a calm voice, "Hey bud, what did you possibly learn from this?"

Steven took a moment to consider what to say in response. Then he smiled and said, "I think I learned that you need to aim away from the window when you try out the Dutch dancer kick."

He saw that I was definitely listening and he added, "I also learned maybe I shouldn't do something like this indoors before thinking it out first."

I am extremely grateful that there are spiritual tools that can help us not follow through on our first impulse to go nuclear on someone who does something upsetting on an already over-filled day. Just that one moment of breathing and asking oneself, "Is my heart open right now," can prevent all sorts of harm and pain that we would later regret (or that your beloved child will tell his or her horrified therapist many times in the future).

The Guilt-Provoking Phone Call
Here's a second quick example of how the phrase "Is my heart open right now" can surprise you with tangible results. You might remember Gayle from earlier in this chapter who admitted how impatient and short-fused she is sometimes with her human loved

ones and how patient, wise, and playful she is consistently with her beloved canine companion.

After we discussed in a few therapy sessions the idea of "circumcising your heart" and asking during a stressful moment, "Is my heart open right now," Gayle soon had a very challenging opportunity to try out this unconventional method in real life.

Here's what happened: Gayle's mom tends to be (like many people we know and love) frequently anxious and quite demanding. Gayle describes how, "My mother starts nearly every phone call or visit by saying with a guilt-provoking tone of voice, 'I've been wondering what happened to you. I haven't heard from you in a while. How come you never call?' Even if it's only been 24 hours since we talked on the phone or saw each other, my mom still has to stick in a little jab each time that implies, 'You don't call enough,' 'You don't love me enough,' 'You're not a very good daughter.'"

In Gayle's rational mind, she knows she does call her mom quite often and that she does love her mom a lot (despite their frequent conflicts). Gayle also has a pretty good sense that she has been a decent and loyal daughter for her mom, especially during all the years since Gayle's father died.

So the issue is not about what is true or rational. Rather, as in most family conflicts, the pain Gayle feels during each phone call or visit with her never-quite-satisfied mom is the reflexive tightening in Gayle's gut, the tension in Gayle's shoulders and neck muscles, and the feeling of wanting to shut down and harden her own heart to protect herself against constantly being told things that imply, "You don't call enough, you don't love me enough, you're not a very good daughter."

A few days after we practiced in a counseling session how to utilize the quick question, "Is my heart open right now," Gayle got a phone call from her mother right in the middle of a stressful day when Gayle was handling four things at once.

Gayle's mother began to say, "I've been wondering what happened to you. I haven't heard from you lately. How come you never call?" Gayle felt her insides starting to get twisted up in knots.

But this time Gayle took a breath and quickly tried out the silent line, "Is my heart open right now." A few days later at her next counseling session, Gayle told me what happened at that moment.

She explained, "It was surprising. Normally I would feel all defensive and try to convince my mother that we did talk yesterday and that I am actually a decent daughter with some redeeming human qualities. But this time I could just focus for a moment on whether or not my heart was opening and I began to notice something new and different. In just a few seconds, I was no longer feeling under attack or in need of defending myself. I started to feel some compassion for how much my mom is helplessly flooded with anxious thoughts and I also began to have some empathy for how clumsy my mom is at asking for what she needs. My mom never learned how to get her needs met in a direct way. She's from the generation that always had to be manipulative or indirect in order to get things done."

Gayle added, "As soon as my heart started to open, I felt a lot freer and less agitated than I've ever felt during a phone call or visit with my mom. I can't change the way she pulls out the guilt card during every conversation. But I realized I could successfully change the way I feel inside and that I can experience my mom with much more caring and patience. For the rest of that phone call, I made sure to keep my heart open and to trust that I didn't need to fix my mom or make her be different from who she is. I could just love her and listen to her for a few minutes without having my energy sapped by her clumsy comments. I got off the phone feeling a lot more centered and alive, which is extremely different from how it used to be each time we had a mother-daughter conversation."

Why Does This Work So Successfully?
From a psychological perspective, what you are achieving when you open up your caring and receptivity by calming yourself with the phrase "Is my heart open right now" is a basic principle called "reciprocal inhibition" that was identified and researched in the 1950's by psychiatrist Joseph Wolpe as an effective way to reinforce something positive and de-activate something self-defeating or harmful. He got the idea for teaching "reciprocal inhibition" to anxious or stressed individuals after Wolpe studied how muscles work in the human body. If you activate one muscle group to move or take action, it tends to cause the opposing muscle group to de-activate.

Similarly in psychology, "reciprocal inhibition" (saying yes to one specific action and thus saying no to its opposite) has been demonstrated repeatedly as a way to activate one set of emotional responses (such as opening up your heart and compassion) and this positive action step tends to calm or de-activate the opposite emotional response (such as being impatient or hostile toward the other person).

In 12-step programs (such as Alcoholics Anonymous or Overeaters Anonymous), this phenomenon of choosing a positive action step (asking yourself "Is my heart open right now" and choosing to do something of service or something compassionate) can quickly shift your energy from its opposite action step (feeling shut down, isolated, or numbing out with an addictive substance) and it's called "taking a contrary action." In 12-step programs it has been shown repeatedly that if you are feeling stuck or repetitive in something self-defeating or harmful, one successful strategy is to take the "contrary action" and do the opposite healthy action with deep intention.

Basically, "reciprocal inhibition" and "contrary action" mean that you can't possibly go in two opposite directions at the exact same moment. You and your body will either move toward an opening of your heart or a closing/numbing of your heart—you get to decide which direction you want to favor during a tense or stressful moment.

It's like the Yiddish expression, "You can't dance at two weddings with one tukhis." During a tense conversation or a challenging moment, you can either dance to the tune of an open heart or you can fold your arms, tighten your jaw, and harden your heart. But you can't move toward opening up and move toward closing down at the exact same moment. (Unless you have two tukhises...which would be quite amazing).

What If Your Inner Agitation Just Won't Let You Pry Your Heart Open

Now here's a back-up plan in case you try out what I've described thus far and it doesn't work sufficiently. For the vast majority of people most of the time, the probing question "Is my heart open right now" is usually enough to cause an immediate shift in your caring and aliveness. But sometimes it takes an extra boost of sincere intention and focus to get the heart to re-open.

For instance, if you tend to be someone who usually needs a few hours or even a few days to cool down when someone upsets you or contradicts you, then you might need something extra to help you make a quick shift from impatience/defensiveness to openness/compassion. Or if your inner agitation becomes especially strong when you are in a tense situation, you will probably need an extra ounce of support and clarity to make the crucial shift from feeling defensive to feeling open and creative again. Sometimes you just need to respect the fact if you are a passionate, fiery, or intense human being, then the process of cooling yourself down might require something extra and reassuring.

For example, a highly-intelligent and hard-working man named Andrew came to one of my speeches. He liked the idea of "circumcising your heart" and he was hopeful about asking the silent line

"Is my heart open right now" during a tense moment at home or at work.   So he tried it out a few times with mixed results.

A few weeks later, Andrew wrote me an email and later came in for a consultation where he described how, "I am usually able to learn things quickly and do them successfully.   But not when it comes to emotions. Something happens when I'm in an argument or a control battle with my wife or my strong-willed daughter that causes me to go ballistic every so often.   I tried saying to myself, 'Is my heart open right now.' But my brain kept racing with argumentative thoughts and a desire to prove how right I am and how wrong they are."

He added, "My wife and my daughter have told me, 'You're a great guy most of the time, but in an argument or a disagreement, you sometimes turn into this rigid, uncompromising pain in the butt.'"

Over the next few weeks during some honest and clarifying counseling sessions, I learned a lot of valuable information about why Andrew tended to get so worked up and unable to cool down during many of his arguments with his wife and his daughter. Andrew had been raised by a highly-critical father and a mother who was a devoted caregiver for Andrew's physically-challenged younger brother Bruce.   No matter what Andrew achieved in school or in sports, his parents kept pressuring him to achieve even more and they gave most of their tenderness, love and patience to Andrew's troubled younger brother Bruce.

As a result, Andrew recalls, "I always felt a little bit overlooked or unappreciated.   I basically had to fight and strive for every important thing in my life.   So when my wife or my daughter need me to be patient, calm, or gentle during a disagreement or a clash of strong wills, I just can't cool down that quickly.   There's a surge of adrenalin and a racing feeling inside me that wants to yell at them, 'Hey, just shut up and let me handle this how I need to handle it. Stop getting in my way!'"

Like many smart and decent people I have met who have strong, fiery emotions, Andrew knew he wanted to be less reactive and explosive. But the racing, agitated feeling he experienced whenever someone criticized him, contradicted him, or pressured him was extremely hard to manage.

In one of our counseling sessions, I asked Andrew, "If you were unable to find a way to cool down more quickly and be less intense and argumentative during a disagreement with your wife or your daughter, what do you think might happen?"

Andrew grew quiet for a moment and then he said softly, "I think they would eventually tune me out or they would want to get away from me entirely. Sometimes I worry that my daughter will move out and not look back once she's old enough to be on her own. Or that my wife is already planning her exit strategy each time I flare up at her and try to wear her down with my arguments and my defensiveness. Both my wife and my daughter have enough self-worth and sanity to know they won't put up with our power struggles and verbal explosions going on like this forever. If I don't get a handle on this, it's going to cost me enormously."

During the next few seconds, I saw Andrew's face become more vulnerable, open and unguarded than I'd ever seen previously in our counseling sessions. He seemed to be making a crucial decision and then he looked directly into my eyes as he said, "We've got to make sure I don't keep pushing them away with my impatience and my anger. I don't want to lose these two people that I love so much."

So together we began to practice an extra self-soothing line that I often recommend to people who have trouble cooling down during an argument or a battle over "who's right and who's wrong" with a spouse or a strong-willed child.

The extra line which Andrew began to say to himself whenever he was feeling worked up, criticized or argumentative with his wife or his daughter was, "This person cares about me and the sooner we both listen to each other's different ideas with an open heart, the sooner we can come up with something useful that both of us can support."

You will notice this extra line has three segments:

- "This person cares about me": reminding yourself that this loved one is not the enemy, but rather is a person who most of the time cares about you (even if he or she recently said or did something you absolutely didn't like at all).
- "The sooner we both listen to each other's different ideas with an open heart": reminding yourself that the fastest way to break the endless debate of who's at fault or who started the tension between the two of you is to just breathe and open up your heart so you can take turns listening to the fact that both of you need to be heard and understood for your differing ideas and perspectives. Both of you are smart people and both of you have a piece of the big picture, so you will need to listen calmly to each other in order to find out the extra information which your own self-righteous point of view hasn't fully appreciated yet.
- "The sooner we can come up with something useful that both of us can support": reminding yourself that as soon as you start listening as teammates and caring souls, you will probably be able to come up with some options that both of you can support and enjoy. It's not a question of who's right or who started the tension, but rather how much you can honor each other's differing insights and come up with some creative solution that honors each person's particular needs and concerns.

A few days later, Andrew had an opportunity to try out this extra line with his family. His wife and his daughter were upset that Andrew had failed to recycle some plastics and glass bottles. So they commented to Andrew, "Don't you care about the environment."

Andrew noticed his blood starting to boil and his mind racing with thoughts like, "Don't tell me what to do" and "Don't talk to me in a condescending tone of voice." There had been many previous arguments and rants in their family about what Andrew called, "The Endless Green Compliance Wars."

But instead of being argumentative or verbally aggressive this time, Andrew took a breath and said to himself, "These people care about me and the sooner we each listen to one another's different ideas with an open heart, the sooner we can come up with something useful that all of us can support."

Andrew recalls feeling a subtle inner shift at that moment. He told me later, "I was almost ready to start lecturing them about how controlling and preachy they tend to be. But I caught myself when I remembered that my wife does care about me and my daughter does care about me. Yes, they are a bit obsessed with saving the planet and recycling 100% of whatever stuff we buy or use. But I decided not to turn this into a power struggle or a battle over who's right and who's wrong."

Andrew felt his heart open a little when he admitted to himself that his wife and his daughter are two of the most caring and loving people he's ever known. So he was able to stay open and calm without a chip on his shoulder this time as he, his wife, and his daughter brainstormed on what could be a good creative option for their family.

As Andrew described, "Thankfully, we didn't waste a lot of time and energy arguing or accusing each other as we usually tend to do. Because we didn't go to war this time for a day or a week over who was right and who was wrong, we only needed about ten minutes to come up with a sensible solution. I offered that I was willing to improve by 70% the amount of stuff I recycle and I asked calmly if they were willing to reduce by 50% the amount of preachiness and pushiness in their tone of voice whenever we were discussing these 'save the world' issues. My wife and my daughter are smart—they know they tend to get a bit self-righteous about recycling and other issues. So they thought the request for 50% less preachiness was sufficiently generous on my part."

Andrew concluded, "I think what's most important is that we were able this time to talk to each other as teammates and creative, smart people who love one another. After years of ugly time-consuming arguments over stuff like this, it felt great that I was able to open up my heart enough to be able to problem-solve with them in a calm and caring way. I think that if I keep cooling myself down this way, then I won't have to mess up the most important relationships in my life. I don't want to lose my wife or my daughter just because I have a lot of fire and intensity inside me."

Finding Your Best De-Escalating Words

Think about it. When you were reading the example of Andrew snapping at his loved ones and being concerned that he doesn't want to lose them or alienate them, did it sound like any situation you are facing at home, at work, or with a family member? Is there someone you care about who has become a little more distant from you because they have been snapped at unintentionally one or more times? Even if you are an essentially kind and caring human being, is there someone in your life who has been on the receiving end of some impatient words or facial gestures from you...and you don't want this to keep happening in the future?

Try out these heart-opening, silent phrases and see if they work for you personally to make sure you don't injure anyone with your impatience, sarcasm, or edginess. Or please be creative and come up with some other specific, self-soothing words and calm reassurances that could work for you personally to cool down quickly when you're feeling impatient, self-righteous or argumentative. You might need to try out several different versions (either on your own or with a counselor or friend) until you find the exact heart-opening phrase that works dependably and effectively for you during a tense moment when you are tempted to be harsh or dismissive to someone who needs your caring and kindness.

Even if you have some extremely legitimate reasons why you've closed down a part of your heart over the years (and thereby shut down a part of your aliveness), please see what you can do to open up once again to the joy, the teamwork, and the companionship you have been missing. Your life, your health, and your most important relationships at home and at work will benefit if you put this spiritual method to good use starting today or very soon.

CHAPTER 3

FINDING A HEALTHY BALANCE

in Situations That Could Rattle You

If you were asked to describe how much you tend to be a "push-over" or a "rigid toughie," what would you say about yourself:

- "In certain situations (whether at work, as a parent, in a love relationship, or with your aging parents) I sometimes become a complete pushover."
- Or, "In certain situations (at work, with family members, in a marriage or relationship) I sometimes come off as a rigid toughie."
- Or, "There are times when I get pulled from one extreme to the other, never quite finding the healthy balance between being too flexible or too firm."

I've found as a therapist that what rattles most men and women who have busy lives is not so much that their schedules are full, but rather that there are difficult choices and dilemmas nearly every day about how much to be flexible and go along with what others want, versus how much to be firm, stubbornly unique, and impervious to what others want you to be.

For example, see how many of these dilemmas sound like you or someone you know:

- On a busy day when you're already doing too much, the phone rings and it's someone you care about who is needing your full attention. What do you do at that moment?
- During a busy week when you're finally able to focus on something important and timely, there's an email or a text asking you to stop what you're doing and show up for some meeting or crisis you had hoped could be resolved without your direct involvement. What are your options for how you would like to respond?
- On a day off when you are hoping to unwind and recharge your energy, you find out someone needs you to help on a project or a personal problem that just can't wait. What is your first reaction to this interruption of your cherished time off?
- In your role as a parent, or in your relationships, or in your work life, or when you volunteer on a heartfelt endeavor, do you ever take on too much responsibility and it starts to wear you down physically or emotionally?
- When you are with a partner or a group that is making a decision about what to do next or how to get something done, do you ever find yourself unable to negotiate well and you wind up either giving in uncomfortably or standing your ground a little too harshly?

Finding the balance between being too accommodating to others, or on the other hand being too stubborn in pursuit of your own agenda, is not easy for most of us. What comes to mind for you as a moment when you felt tugged upon like the wishbone at a Thanksgiving dinner, being pulled in two directions at once? What's it like inside your noisy brain, your tightened gut, or your frayed nerve endings when you feel conflicted between the urge to be "generous, helpful and flexible" and the equally strong urge to be "firm, resolute, and stand your ground."

The Steps for Finding the Balance Between the Extremes of "Too Nice" or "Too Rigid"
One of the things I love about Jewish spirituality is how psychologically astute and highly-practical it tends to be. This is especially true on the topic of finding the healthy balance between being too flexible and being too rigid or inflexible.

Many centuries ago, the Jewish Kabbalists (the word "Kabbalah" means "received wisdom," "mystical teachings," or "deeper levels of interpretation of the Hebrew scriptures") admitted that we humans cannot know for certain how God or the Ultimate Source operates in the universe, but we can look at some of the strongest energies flowing all around us and within us to get some clues. Some of these energies seem like irreconcilable opposites, but the Kabbalists showed how certain contrasting flows of energy can blend together and harmonize in fascinating and useful ways.

For example, two of the strongest energies of how the universe operates and they seem at first to be irreconcilable opposites, are:

1) There seem to be strong flows of loving-kindness, which in Hebrew is called Chesed (pronounced khesed with a gentle throat-clearing khh), and
2) There also seem to be many strong flows of the contrasting energy of limit-setting, firmness, or structure, which in Hebrew is called Gevurah.

When you are fully present with an adorable baby, or the warm hands of your beloved, or the nourishing wind that causes the plants to spread their seeds and grow, or the boundless concern you feel for someone or something that deeply touches your heart, or the desire to be part of the healing and repair of some aspect of the world, you are experiencing a flow of Chesed or loving-kindness. When you set up a limit, a fence, a boundary, a rule, a structure, a habit, a ritual, a vessel, or a container that holds or directs something and keeps it from being scattered or chaotic, then you are experiencing the contrasting energy of Gevurah.

Now here's where it gets interesting and very useful for finding balance in your everyday life. The Kabbalists theorized a vision of how the world works and in this vision (which they call The Tree of Life or the 10 Sephirot or divine emanations) there is a multi-dimensional grid of constantly flowing energies moving around us and within us. It's somewhat like the multi-dimensional grid a scientist might envision of electromagnetic energies that flow in various directions around the Earth and in our muscles and nerves. Or the multi-dimensional grid of life-force energy or Chi that you would see posted on the wall if you went into an acupuncturist's office and looked at the meridians and chakras of the human body.

There have been several hundred books, chapters and website articles written about the Kabbalistic idea of 10 key energy flows and how they function in our emotions, our personality traits, and our daily dilemmas. In fact, there have been more books, chapters, and articles written about this thought-provoking spiritual topic than there have been TV episodes of "Seinfeld," "Big Bang Theory," and "Downton Abbey" all added together, although you wouldn't know it just by looking at the program guide on your television.

In the Kabbalistic view of how things work, you need a good amount of loving-kindness (Chesed) and a good amount of Gevurah (limits, structures, and containers) in order for life to be balanced and highly-functional. Sadly, if you are without much love or kindness in your daily interactions for an extended amount of time, it's bound to hurt, cause conflicts, or drain your life-force. Or, on the other hand, imagine if you are without any limits, structures or containers for all your energy and impulsiveness--it could result in lots of chaotic, scattered, easily distracted, or messy moments. We need flows of loving-kindness (Chesed) in order to build and sustain families, relationships, communities, creative work partnerships, and heartfelt involvements to worthy causes. We also need limits and structures (Gevurah) to make sure we don't get stuck in randomness, chaos, endless detours, or scattered efforts that never turn into something tangible and fulfilling.

In addition to exploring these basic life-enhancing energies that can make us more fully alive and highly-functional, the Kabbalists also realized that too much of a good thing can sometimes be a problem. For instance, if there is nothing but unfiltered flows of Chesed (loving-kindness) pouring forth with no boundaries or containment, then it can easily throw us out of balance and become a series of problems. To illustrate this idea of "excessive flows of Chesed/loving-kindness", take a moment to ask yourself:

- Have you ever been so head over heels passionately in love with an idea or a person that you were unable to think clearly or stay in alignment with your core truth and values?
- Have you ever been so loving and so caring toward someone who was relying on you a lot that you inadvertently blocked this person's attempts to find his or her own strength and your unintentional "smothering love" might have hampered this person's necessary steps toward greater independence and self-worth?
- Have you ever been so passionately involved in a cause, a project, a business, or a non-profit goal that you became oblivious to your own health needs or the legitimate needs of someone in your personal life who was feeling ignored?
- Have you ever felt so swept up in your heartfelt efforts to pursue an unattainable person or an unattainable goal that you forgot to take care of some basic details in your

personal life, such as paying the bills, washing the dishes, getting enough sleep, or watching out for the uneven lifted parts of the sidewalk pavement that caused you to trip and fall?

On the other extreme, the Kabbalists have demonstrated that leaning too much in the direction of Gevurah (limit-setting, rules, structures) can also knock you off balance and cause problems. Consider for a moment:

- Have you ever been in a relationship or a workplace where the other person you were dealing with on a daily basis was so consumed by details, rules, procedures, or micro-managing small things and as a result the joy and the humanity of the situation got diminished?
- Have you ever been in a family, an organization or a social situation where there was so much emphasis on the outer forms, hallowed traditions, or "proper way of doing things" and as a result there was a failure to respond to some genuine human needs or some opportunities to change and grow?
- Have you ever been so locked in by your own habits and routines that you were unable to be flexible and graceful in a situation that required some flexibility of thinking or action?
- Have you ever found yourself in a relationship or a work situation becoming defensive or grouchy because someone wanted you to loosen up or give them some room to breathe?

Finding the Beauty of the Balance
In the Jewish spiritual teachings about how the universe and how the individual can flow with greater alignment and vitality,

there is a fascinating next step once you discover you are leaning too much in the direction of either Chesed (unlimited love) or Gevurah (endless amounts of structure and forms). On the multi-dimensional grid of nourishing energies called the Tree of Life, these two opposite polarities can blend or synthesize in an exciting new harmony or convergence called "Tiferet", a Hebrew word that means beauty, balance, adornment, or integration.

When I think of the word Tiferet, I think of a beautiful vessel that can add a little extra joy, goodness, or meaning as it channels or carries the energies of something delightful and nourishing. For example, if you poured endless amounts of healthy herbal tea and you didn't have a functional or beautiful vessel to hold it or transport it, the tea would just be a scattered, chaotic puddle or mess. But if you come up with a Tiferet (balanced) synthesis, then you will set your sights on something harmonious and highly-functional such as a beautiful glass or cup that enhances the tea experience and allows the tea to be used in life-affirming ways. In a Tiferet (balanced) outcome, the adornment of the container or structure (the aesthetics of the beautiful cup holding the tea and the calm, gentle way you pour it and drink from it) actually increases the goodness and meaning of whatever is flowing inside the container or structure.

What Jewish spirituality and Kabbalistic theorists have shown us is that each seemingly out of balance moment is possibly a Tiferet (integrative) opportunity if we choose to be creative and mindful enough to make it so.

Taking the Next Step
Now let's see how this ancient wisdom about finding balance applies to a stressful moment in your life today or later this week. Here's what you can do as a quick mindfulness practice to bring this spiritual method of harmony and alignment into your daily life:

During a tense moment on an over-packed day or right in the middle of a challenging situation, take a few seconds to open yourself up to the energetic qualities of Tiferet (beauty, balance, integration, harmony, adornment, blending the best of two opposing energies into a new form). Start by taking a few calm, gentle breaths as you open up your heart and mind to receive some important insight about how to find the balance or "sweet spot" between the part of you that leans too much toward being "too nice" and the contrasting part of you that occasionally holds on very intensely toward rigid habits or structures that might sometimes need a little more flexibility or kindness.

I've found with numerous diverse counseling clients and in my own life that you can do this quickly, effectively, and creatively by asking yourself three short questions in any high-stress moment of conflict or during any tough decisions:

Question 1: What would be a "too nice" or "overly generous" way to deal with this situation?

Question 2: What would be a "too harsh," "too rigid," or "too cold" way to deal with this situation?

Question 3: What is a creative and life-affirming way to have a balance (Tiferet) that has a good amount of loving-kindness (Chesed) and a good amount of form and structure (Gevurah)?

To help you understand the specifics of how to start using this spiritual method during any of your stressful moments, here are a few examples of Tiferet (balance and beauty) when it is successfully blending together the best aspects of the two polarities of Chesed (unbounded loving-kindness) and Gevurah (strong limit-setting). See which of these sound like something you already do well and which are some possible results that you would like to be able to do successfully in the near future:

Example #1: The Concerned Mom and the Intense Teen
One of my counseling clients is a smart and hard-working woman named Margaret who has a very intense and strong-willed 15 year old daughter named Jessica. Recently Margaret found out from a

mom in their after-school carpool that Jessica and her four clos-est friends have been invited to a dance party next weekend at the home of a girl from her school. Margaret's carpool friend implied there might be alcohol and drugs at the party, which Jessica had said a few days ago was "just a little sleepover with four girls at their friend's house."

Margaret was terrified that Jessica was going to lose her excel-lent grades and her extra-curricular activities if she attended the party and started getting involved with any stoners or drinkers at her school. Margaret was also upset that Jessica had mis-represent-ed the details of the party to her and that this pattern of "shading the truth" was causing their formerly strong mother-daughter re-lationship to become a stubborn power struggle of angry debates and increasing distrust.

According to Margaret, "In the past few months, Jessica and I have had several of these ugly battles. I try to be her ally and her confidante, but each time when I sense she is lying to me, I end up yelling at her and sometimes grounding her for a week. Or taking away her cell phone for a few days, which doesn't do much except to push Jessica farther away and make her even more sneaky and dishonest. That's exactly what I don't want to happen this time."

Jessica was terrified that her mother was going to forbid her from attending the party or that Margaret might ground her for once again hiding the truth and getting caught in a lie. According to Jessica, "My mom used to be super nice and understanding, but lately she's become very controlling and rigid. It makes me afraid to tell her the truth and we wind up yelling and arguing each time I get caught making stuff up to calm her fears."

Like many people who love each other but who have trouble saying no to one another or setting up healthy limits, Margaret and her daughter Jessica were both feeling frustrated and exasper-ated. So we looked at the Jewish spiritual method of finding the Tiferet possibilities (balance, beauty, harmony, and envisioning the creative synthesis between being "too nice" or "too rigid"). Was there some way to turn the stressful power struggle sparked by this party invitation into a positive chance for learning, growing, and strengthening the bond of love and trust between Margaret and her daughter Jessica?

In my office, I asked Margaret to have an open mind and an open heart as she sat down with Jessica and explored calmly as teammates the three questions listed earlier. The goal was not to have one of them win and one of them lose. The goal was to be creative and innovative in coming up with a beautiful, balanced solution that honored both the desire for loving-kindness and the desire for limits that made sense to both of them.

As a first step, Margaret and Jessica talked calmly about Question 1: "What would be an example of 'too nice' or 'overly generous' in this situation."

Jessica spoke up right away and said, "That's easy. I think if my mom caved like she usually does, that would be totally lame and weak. My mom yells a lot and threatens to take things away, but half the time if I get upset enough and dramatic enough she caves."

Margaret agreed, as she explained, "Jessica's right. I tend to fluctuate between being the nice all-giving parent who doesn't want my daughter to be angry with me. Or I flip to the other extreme and I start yelling at her about her sneakiness or taking away her cell phone for a few days, but then I go back on my word and I try to win Jessica back by being all nice and compliant again."

Then Margaret and Jessica explored Question 2: "What would be an example of 'too rigid' or 'too harsh' in this situation." Margaret answered first, "I think it would be too rigid if I grounded Jessica for a month because she lied to me about the party being just a sleepover with a few of her friends when in fact it's going to be a big risky party with all sorts of entitled kids who have parents that never say no. Of course I'm tempted to ground her for a year for being such a sneak, yet I know in my heart that my biggest desire is not to push her further into defiance, but rather to open up communication, trust and honesty again like we used to have not too long ago."

Jessica replied, "Yeah, I think whether you ground me for a day, or a week, or a month is not the issue we need to resolve. I think if you want me to stop lying and keeping things from you, then you need to start listening with a little more caring and concern when I do try to tell you things. For instance, I've told you more than once that I think my friends who drink and do drugs make fools of themselves and they often throw up on their boyfriend's front seats. Plus the fact that Dad was a drinker who sometimes got totally mean when he had one too many. I've told you I don't want to drink or do drugs and I wish you would take my words seriously. And just because I dress a little edgy sometimes doesn't make me a problem child or a depressed Goth. It's just some fun I like to have sometimes trying on different characters with the way I dress."

Margaret took a breath and carefully listened this time to her daughter. With her eyes and with her words, Margaret said, "I love you Jess and you are an amazing person. And I do believe you when you say you don't want to drink or do drugs. But you've got to appreciate the fact that it's scary to let you go to a party where there will be all sorts of peer pressure on you to do things that could disrupt all the good things you've been accomplishing at school."

Jessica smiled as she replied, "Yeah, I get it. Life is scary and your little girl is growing up."

Now Margaret and Jessica were ready for Question 3: "What would be a creative and life-affirming way in this situation to find a balance that has a good amount of loving-kindness (Chesed) and a good amount of form and structure (Gevurah)?"

This third question took a few minutes before Margaret and Jessica came up with a win-win balanced solution they both could live with. Jessica had suggested at first that she could be trusted to go to the party and not drink or do drugs. Margaret admitted she wanted to trust Jessica, but she also didn't want to be a pushover or to send her daughter into a complicated situation with lots of peer pressure and no clear-cut plan for what to do and how to stay strong and safe if things got strange at the party.

Then Margaret suggested Jessica could say no to the risky party and invite three or four of her friends to sleep over at Jessica's house that night. Jessica said that wouldn't work because her four closest friends were all going to the party.

Finally, Jessica offered a creative and balanced solution that Margaret liked a lot. It happened after Margaret said calmly and lovingly to her daughter, "I hope you can see that this is not a battle over who's got control and who's going to be the one to give in. This is about the two of us making sure you don't give up your voice, your strength, your health, and your successes in school because some cute guy comes up to you and offers you something to drink or smoke. You and I both want the same things—we want you to be an amazing young woman who doesn't get mistreated or pressured by anyone. We both want you to be safe and strong."

Jessica then spoke up and said, "Mom, I've got a crazy idea. Why don't we have my four friends come over here an hour before the party and the five of us can talk about how we're gonna have each other's backs at the party. We can come up with a code word that says someone is pressuring one of us or that we need the others to stay close by because some creep at the party is not taking no for an answer."

Margaret asked, "At this 'Do You Have Each Other's Back' conversation, am I allowed to offer some suggestions, too?"

Jessica thought for a moment and replied, "Just a few suggestions, not a whole lecture, o.k. It would be dorky if my mom was running the show and I was just a wimpy do-gooder."

Margaret decided to say yes to Jessica's balanced solution of a "Do You Have My Back" conversation with Jessica's four friends. As Margaret told me later, "I felt relieved that Jessica was willing to get her friends involved in making sure each of them was going to be safe and supported if something got confusing or dangerous at the party. Since I can't be there to watch everything and make sure they are o.k., this felt like a decent way to help Jessica get in touch with what it means to be a healthy, supportive posse of young women watching out for each other in the wilds of Southern California. There are no guarantees, but it feels good to know she and her friends are alerting each other to the dangers and how to deal with those dangers."

What Margaret and Jessica accomplished by exploring together the three questions of "too nice," "too rigid" and "balanced with a good amount of loving-kindness and limit-setting" is that they shifted their mother-daughter energy from a power struggle and instead began to build a more creative and teamwork-oriented way of relating to each other.

Margaret told me during a later counseling session that she and Jessica now take a few minutes every week or two to sit down and brainstorm together on how to find a balanced solution to various dilemmas that come up at school, in social situations, and in their home life. According to Margaret, "I'm seeing a lot of growth in Jessica. Instead of becoming a defiant sneak or putting up walls toward me, Jessica seems to be feeling respected and appreciated by me, which gives her the confidence to open up and admit when she needs extra support to handle some of the challenges she's been facing each week."

Example #2:   The Neatnik and the Oblivious Roommate
Caroline and her boyfriend Daniel had been doing great together until Daniel moved into her apartment and they began to clash over the issue of how to keep the place clean and organized. As you will find in many otherwise compatible couples, one of the

partners (Caroline) was very concerned about coming home each day to a neat environment with no dirty dishes or messy piles of clutter, while the other partner (Daniel) was mostly unaware or not very concerned about cleaning up each day.

As Daniel admitted, "I'm the kind of person who will do a huge cleanup if we've got company coming over or parents visiting. But the rest of the time, I just like to relax and not worry about that stuff."

To which Caroline replied, "I'm not claiming to be right or wrong, but coming home to dishes in the sink or piles of unsorted mail, papers, and dirty clothes makes me want to scream. I never thought I'd be living like this."

When the arguments about neatness and messiness got worse and threatened to destroy their relationship, Daniel and Caroline came in for a few counseling sessions. After hearing the reasons why both of them felt strongly about their differing points of view, I asked them if they'd be willing to act as "Brainstorming Teammates" in utilizing the three question approach described earlier. Here's what happened:

- On the question of what would be "too nice" or "too generous," Caroline felt it would be awkward or uncomfortable for her to give in and let Daniel's messy, oblivious style set the tone in their apartment. Daniel felt it would be "too nice" if he used up an hour of his free time each night to do the fastidious cleanup that Caroline required.
- On the question of what would be "too rigid," "too harsh," or "too cold" in this situation, Daniel and Caroline both agreed that they needed to stop being so sarcastic and shaming in the way they talked to each other about messiness and cleanliness. As Daniel described, "When I get sarcastic or I call Caroline a 'Neat Freak' or a 'Nag,' I can see it hurts her and that's not what I want. It's too harsh

when I call her insulting names and in fact I do appreciate that she has a beautiful sense of style and presentation in all areas of her life. That's one of the things I've always found attractive about her and I guess if she's got a strong aesthetic sense at work and in the way she dresses, it makes sense that she'd have a strong aesthetic sense about her living space as well."

Caroline offered, "I also need to stop using shaming words like 'slob' or 'clueless' or 'roommate from hell' when I talk to Daniel about things that feel chaotic or messy at home. If I call him names, I'm not only making the situation worse but I'm also setting a precedent for him to call me things I don't want to be called."

- On the question of what would be a Tiferet (balanced, harmonious, integrative, beautiful) solution, Caroline and Daniel came up with several creative options including the following solution that they agreed to put into practice right away.

Daniel had suggested, "If there's good music playing in the background and no bossy tone of voice from Caroline, I can do about ten or fifteen minutes each morning before I go to work and each night when I get home to make sure my clothes aren't on the floor and my dishes aren't in the sink. On weekends, I'm willing to do a half hour of heavy duty cleanup if we add the music and the sense of fun to it. My goal is to not make it a rigid chore, but rather to make it something enjoyable we do together with music, laughter, and some playfulness."

Caroline agreed, "I've always been a bit of a task-master with myself and others, but if Daniel wants to help me lighten up and add a little fun and music to the daily cleanup ritual, I'm all for it. As long as I feel we're teammates and we're helping each other out because we love each other, I can take some of the harsh and rigid tone out of the way I approach daily organizing and cleaning.   I might actually enjoy the music and the playfulness that Daniel is adding to our life together.   It's a lot better than having to do it all myself or resenting him more and more."

As Caroline and David discovered, the Tiferet (balanced) solution is not about transforming your partner into an entirely different person.   It's simply a chance to honor who you both are and to turn the power struggle into a chance to be more lovable, alive, creative, and connected.   Daniel is still a lot less concerned about neatness than Caroline tends to be.   But the two of them are now aligned in an enjoyable daily way of making the domestic teamwork fun and filled with their favorite music.

Example #3:   The Overloaded Do-Gooder and the Feeling of "It's Never Enough"

Now we come to a dilemma that nearly every temple, synagogue, church, non-profit group, condo association, co-op board, school committee, and charitable organization encounters quite often. It seems to be customary in nearly every do-gooder setting that there are a few intensely overloaded staff or volunteers, while the vast majority of members are doing very little to keep things going.

For instance, Roberta is a deeply compassionate and very competent person who nonetheless gets overloaded sometimes by saying yes to a growing list of important involvements. Like many genuinely caring people, she often says yes to lots of projects and caregiving situations, even when her own health suffers or the other important priorities and goals in her life get pushed aside or put on hold.

When I first met Roberta at one of my workshops on "Stress and Overload Remedies for Non-profit Volunteers and Staff," she told me during a snack break conversation, "I almost didn't get here today. I signed up a few weeks ago, but in the past 48 hours

I've had two family crises and one emergency board meeting at my congregation that initially got scheduled for today but then it got re-scheduled for tomorrow. It seems whenever I think I have a moment to do something positive and healing for myself, it gets interrupted by some crisis that is beyond my control."

Roberta added, "I was recently told by one of my doctors that the reason I frequently come down with a cold, the flu, or digestive problems might be that I'm not able to sort out and release all the intense personalities and dilemmas I deal with each week in my work at a non-profit, in my family where I am the caregiver for someone with intense physical and emotional challenges, and in my congregation where I'm on the board and we're going through some painful cutbacks and budget crises."

To help Roberta and others find a healthy balance between "being too generous to others" and "being too rigid or cut-off from things you genuinely want to help support," we explored that afternoon how to use the quick three question method for balancing Chesed (loving-kindness) and Gevurah (setting limits for yourself and others).

In Roberta's situation, none of her options for "cutting back" or "focusing on her own health" seemed do-able at first. Roberta felt strongly that she didn't want to abandon her commitment to her family member who has special needs and requires lots of help. Nor did Roberta want to cut back on her commitment to her non-profit work, which is vitally important to her and to the community she serves. Nor did Roberta want to cut back on her commitment to her congregation, where she had spent several years waiting for the chance to become a board member and make an impact on programming, membership, and other issues she was hoping to improve during a time of budget cuts and tough choices.

But Roberta also knew, "Just thinking about the insane amount of stuff that's piled up on my 'To Do' list each week gives me a headache sometimes and often keeps me up at night. I'm frequently feeling, 'How did I get into all this and why do I feel that no matter how much I do it's never quite enough?'"

Does that sound like you or someone you know? Is there a current overload of people expecting things from you or relying on you to handle complicated situations that invariably take more time and energy than you have available? Is there a lingering feeling inside you that no matter what you do there is always a huge list of things you don't have time to address adequately?

Finding a satisfying and creative Tiferet balance that has a good amount of Chesed (loving-kindness) and Gevurah (limit-setting) is a skill that most of us need help in developing. Here's what happened when Roberta asked the three questions that I'm hoping you will ask in order to find the healthy balance that can restore your vitality and enjoyment of the necessary things you do each week:

On the first question of "What would be too generous or too nice," Roberta thought for a moment and then admitted, "I think it's too generous when I rush in and offer to do things without checking with other people to see if maybe there are one or two competent individuals who want to help also. Or when I quickly decide to do things for my family member who has special needs that he can sometimes do for himself. I have this habit of being the female knight in shining armor, rushing in with my solutions and my caring, when in fact sometimes there are people on the sidelines saying, 'Who died and made her God?' Or they are thinking to themselves, 'Why does Roberta think she is the only one who can do this. We're not idiots. If she slowed down and checked in with us, she might find we have some things to contribute as well.'"

On the second question of "What would be 'too cold,' 'too harsh,' or 'too rigid' in this situation?," Roberta was silent for almost a minute and then she got tears in her eyes as she imagined, "It would be so cold and so 'not me' if I had to go around saying

'No,' 'I'm too busy,' or 'I'm burned out—go find someone else' in a harsh or dismissive way. If I'm going to have to cut back even just a little for my health in order to be more balanced and less prone to colds, flus, and other ailments, then I want to be able to say 'No' in a loving way and with genuinely realistic back-up plans so that I don't just bail out on these important commitments. I don't want to be a selfish hard-ass who sets rigid or cold limits. That's just not who I am."

Then Roberta began to brainstorm with one of her friends at the workshop on ways to find a healthy integration, a Tiferet sense of beautiful balance, between the part of her that wanted to be helping people all the time and the part of her that needed to set some healthy limits and not stay in a perpetual state of stress and overload. Roberta thought about various options that didn't feel right to her and then she came up with something that did feel satisfying and true to who she is.

She explained, "I've decided to start being not just the helper all the time but also to find my long-absent voice that can ask for help and inspire others to do what they are capable of doing well. I have several people in my congregation who can sometimes cover for me when I can't be at a meeting or when I can't be doing all the preparation details for every program event. They're smart and capable, but I need to start asking gently, calmly, and lovingly for the support and teamwork that some of these people are very willing and able to give me. The same thing is true at my non-profit work. I can make sure to hold onto the most important tasks that I want to do myself in my own way, but I can also ask for help and teamwork on some of the other more tedious tasks that I've been doing by myself and yet if I let someone help me out it would probably turn out good enough."

Roberta thought about her family member who needs a lot of caregiving and realized, "There are lots of people who can do some of the driving and some of the errands that I've been doing myself and that take up way too much time and energy. I still want to be the person who looks into his eyes, calls him on the phone consistently, and connects with him in a deep way. But I can let go and ask for help and support on some of the time-consuming things that don't require my personal touch."

As with many Tiferet (balanced, integrative) solutions, Roberta was not being asked to go to the extremes of "either do it all yourself" or "let go of all of it and just say no." Rather, she was developing a number of balanced options that had her personal style of kindness and attention to detail, but these solutions also freed up some of her time and reduced her stress because she was allowing others to help out also.

Breaking the Habit of Failing to Ask for Help

Learning how to ask for teamwork and proper back-up is not an easy thing for many people, including myself. I grew up as a caregiver for my mom and for others who were seriously ill. For many years I tended to jump in and do too much in my work, my volunteer activities, and my family responsibilities to the point where my wife commented, "You know, when you don't ask for help and you get grumpy or exhausted it's not all that attractive. How about if you let other people contribute a little and see if you can live with the idea that you don't have to carry it all on your shoulders. Just make sure you ask early, gently, and lovingly, rather than waiting until you're at the end of your rope and you're exasperated or frustrated."

I remember thinking at that moment, "Wow, she is not shy about busting my chops. But she does it lovingly and with true wisdom. I'm very fortunate to have such an honest partner."

During the many years since my wife Linda offered that wisdom about asking for help in a calm and inclusive way, I'll admit I haven't made 100% progress. But I'm told by my wife, my son, and others that I've made maybe 90% progress in learning how to find a balance between doing too much for others or making sure I take good care of my own health and not getting burned out.

How about you? Is there someone in your life who has been saying gently (or not so gently), "Please don't be such a martyr doing too much and then getting grumpy or worn down." You can still do a whole lot more than most human beings while also letting other competent people carry some of the load. Just make sure you ask early, gently, and lovingly, because it's a lot more effective than waiting until you are exasperated and snapping at people in your home or at work with comments like, "Doesn't anyone around here lift a finger" or "How come I always have to be the one to do it all."

It gets easier to ask for help in a calm and loving way if you first take a moment to center yourself by taking a few gentle breaths and then imagining the three quick questions: what would be "too nice and generous," what would be "too rigid, harsh, or cold," and what would be a healthy way of building better teamwork and more mutual support in areas where you've been carrying a painful load all by yourself. I hope you take that moment to center yourself and set healthy limits in a caring and non-accusatory way. You probably will find that at least a few people do want to help lighten your load somewhat if you treat them as a valued teammate rather than as the object of your exasperation and flashes of anger.

CHAPTER 4

ADDRESSING THE FEARS AND
PRESSURES THAT CONSTRICT YOU

Can I ask you a very unusual question: How noisy is your brain?

Obviously, it's less noisy than a car alarm going "Cuckoo for Coco Puffs" just outside your bedroom window. But when you are worried about your health, or you are feeling uncertain about your finances, or ruminating about your children's future, or feeling agitated about a frustrating situation at work or in your extended family, what is the noise like inside your brain? What happens to the rest of your body when your brain is cooking with concerns about whether you will be able to handle what's troubling you? Do you sometimes notice that your stomach, your neck, your jaw, your shoulders, your back, or your hands are tensing up?

Wouldn't it be great if we could be fully rested each night, fully alive each day, and not be knocked off track by excessive worries, self-doubts, and distracting thoughts?

I assume you've already been working on this issue of "quieting the noisy brain" in your own life and making some progress.

But I've found that even the most intelligent and spiritual men and women tend to get stuck in fear or self-doubts every so often and need an extra boost of wisdom and support to get to the next level of freedom from the agitated thoughts that swirl inside most human beings, especially on stressful days or when you're dealing with a tough unresolved situation.

This chapter will explore how to move quickly from a moment of uncertainty or self-doubt and learn how to turn those stuck moments into personal breakthroughs that can make a difference in your own well-being and in the well-being of those you live with, work with, or interact with on a daily basis.

Taking a Quick Personal Inventory
First, let's start with where you are currently with regard to fears, insecurities and agitated thoughts that sometimes might be a problem. Please take a moment to answer honestly:

- Is there some goal or quest in your life that you've been afraid to follow through or explore fully because of some lingering self-doubts or anxious concerns?
- With regard to your health and physical vitality, do you sometimes find yourself filled with more fear, second-guessing, and inconsistent strategies (such as start/stop, start/stop fitness programs) than you wish you had?
- Do you sometimes get caught up in concerns about whether your looks, your financial situation, your kids' behaviors, your own "coolness," or even your personal progress toward enlightenment are "good enough" compared to the people around you?
- In your work life or your volunteer activities, do you sometimes feel as if you are faking it, afraid of being "found out," and can't seem to let your good ideas, your creativity, or your most productive energies emerge?

- In your family situation, do you sometimes find yourself walking on egg shells when dealing with a particular individual who has the habit of saying or doing things that leave you feeling frustrated or knocked off center?
- In your personal friendships and romantic relationships, do you ever feel afraid of being criticized, judged harshly, or left behind and, as a result, you use up a lot of energy "saving face" or doing what others want?

If you answered yes to one or more of the above questions... congratulations! You are definitely a living, breathing human and that's a good thing. If you were so completely blissed out and had none of the above challenges whatsoever, we would have to check to see if you still have a pulse.

Now that you've identified one or more areas where fears and self-doubts are sometimes running the show, you have an excellent opportunity to make some additional progress and learn a powerful and profound method for dealing more effectively with these fears and inner agitations. This life-changing method for overcoming the noisy, anxious brain comes from a Jewish spiritual teacher who lived more than two hundred years ago but whose words and insights continue to inspire millions of Jews and non-Jews worldwide long after he died.

The Seeker Who Found Deep Joy in the Midst of Painful Challenges

According to several biographers, Rabbi Nachman of Bratzlav (located in the Ukraine) was a somewhat fragile and vulnerable human being who nevertheless was revered as a great teacher and community leader during his short lifetime. He was the great-grandson of the Baal Shem Tov, the founder of the Hasidic movement in Judaism. Yet Rabbi Nachman's many followers sought him out not just because of his lineage but because of his honesty, his intense search for life's deeper meanings, and his unrelenting quest to connect with the mysteries of the Divine Presence.

Throughout his life, Rabbi Nachman had to deal frequently with intense depression symptoms, numerous personal losses (including several of his children who died at a very young age and the loss of his wife to tuberculosis in her mid-30's). He often faced severe opposition from other teachers and movements within Judaism during his lifetime. Rabbi Nachman spent the last few years of his life coping with the night sweats, fevers, chills, pain and coughing of tuberculosis that eventually took his life in 1810 at the age of 38.

Yet despite all he faced on a physical and emotional level, Rabbi Nachman discovered each day how to embrace joy and seek profound wisdom. His students and followers preserved many of his most important teachings and insights on how to find joy and connection to the Divine no matter what is happening. Some of Rabbi Nachman's life-affirming quotations include:

"We need to start over each day. And sometimes many times each day."

"If you believe you can damage or harm, then also believe that you can fix."

"Even if you can't sing well, sing. Sing to yourself. Sing in the privacy of your home. But sing."

"Today you can feel uplifted. Do not let yesterday or tomorrow bring you down."

"Prayer depends on the heart. A person should put all of his heart into it, so that you shouldn't be in the aspect of 'With their lips they honor Me, but their hearts are far from Me.' (Isaiah 29)."

Among his most famous quotes is the one that has inspired me and many other people as a mantra or a transformative phrase for shifting out of fear or agitation so that in the middle of a tough situation you can quickly re-awaken your energies for being more alive and conscious. The uplifting quote from Rabbi Nachman of Bratzlav that can help you deal more effectively with moments of fear, self-doubt, or inner agitation is:

Kol ha-olam kulo	All the world
gesher t'sar meh-ohd	is a very narrow bridge.
V'ha-eekar	And above all (or) the main thing (or) the important thing
lo l'fached	is not to fear
k'lal	at all (or) not completely (or) not entirely.

Before we practice using this powerful meditative phrase, let's explore the different ways to understand what it means:

Possibility #1:   Using This Quote as an Aspiration or a Visualization

Most people translate the final word "k'lal" as "at all," which makes the Rabbi Nachman quote: "All the world is a very narrow bridge, and the main thing is not to fear at all."   In Israel a popular song was written several years ago with these words and it has been sung passionately ever since at summer camps, temples, concerts, Jewish spirituality gatherings, and meditation retreats in the United States and worldwide.

But if you think about it, the phrase "not to fear at all" is probably a hope and not an actual reality.   It's an imaginative visualization or a personal inspiration of what it might feel like to be fearless and no longer slowed down by worries, self-doubts, or external obstacles.

Yet even if it's not a current reality, there are many benefits from using an uplifting visualization or an inspirational phrase like this during anxious moments.   For instance, when you say or sing, "All the world is a very narrow bridge and the main thing is not to fear at all," you are suggesting strongly to your mind and your nerve endings that you can truly envision a powerful courage from deep inside your soul that lifts you out of fear and opens you up to going forward fully committed and fully passionate.

What would that be like for you or for someone you care about? What would it feel like to be in a calmly-induced state of "no fear at all?" As you close your eyes for a moment, say the words slowly, breathe calmly in and out, as you imagine a place deep inside you where there is no fear, no pain, no anxieties, no sadness—a place where possibly you are filled with light from a mysterious Source and where you are strengthened by the power of a mysterious Presence.

Imagine yourself feeling able to journey across one of life's narrow bridges with complete confidence and mental clarity. It might take a leap of faith to reach this internal state of "no fear at all," especially when you are feeling sluggish, worn down, or anxious. But like millions of others who have said or sung this powerful phrase during the past two hundred years, see what happens in your own body and mind when you repeat the words of Rabbi Nachman, "All the world is a very narrow bridge, and the main thing is not to fear at all."

Then without judging or criticizing anything, take a moment to acknowledge what happened for you when you attempted to visualize a place deep inside you that is free from fear or self-doubts. What was it like to envision that secure place of fearlessness? Was it easy or difficult to get beyond the skeptical brain and find the courageous, passionate place deep inside you?

Please don't worry if it was unreachable at first. I've found that for many people, saying Rabbi Nachman's phrase and seeking to find a fearless place deep inside is not an immediate slam dunk. Sometimes it takes several attempts to find that place of strength and clarity which is hidden underneath many layers of fear and tension.

What's most important is that you don't give up after only one or two attempts.   If you are a creative person or if you have the ability to visualize deep within your mind's eye, you will probably be successful at finding (after a few more attempts) that a fearless version of yourself is reachable.   Here is a quick example of what can happen if you practice using Rabbi Nachman's phrase in various tough situations:

The Dad Who Was Stuck in Fear
Don is a hard-working engineer with a strong ability to design technical solutions for resolving complex real-world problems.   He also has a great sense of humor and playfulness, especially with his three children.   But he tends to be someone who has trouble talking about feelings.   He is described by his wife Emily as "a good man who is the steady but silent type."

Don was sent to counseling by his wife Emily because (in Emily's words), "Don was shutting down emotionally and freezing up with fear because of the recent crisis in our family."

Specifically, Don and Emily have a son named Jonah who has been diagnosed with cancer and is undergoing various treatments. According to Emily, "Don has always been a devoted and involved dad for our kids.   But the fear of losing Jonah and the horrible frustrations of seeing our son impacted by various chemotherapies has caused Don to become distant, tense, and unreachable."

During our counseling sessions I learned that Don understandably felt very agitated inside because he couldn't "fix" or "solve" his son Jonah's situation.   Don also felt secretly ashamed at how much the fear of losing Jonah was affecting Don's moods and even his ability to focus at work.

As Don admitted to me, "I'm a problem solver at work and I pride myself on coming up with sensible solutions.   It messes with my head that I am so unable right now to help Jonah with his cancer and I'm in such unfamiliar territory dealing with these doctors, lab tests, complex decisions, awful side-effects, and disappointing results. Every time I think there's a ray of hope or a plan of action, it gets taken away or tossed aside because of new factors we hadn't considered previously."

After several counseling sessions in which we explored these feelings of powerlessness and frustration, I asked Don if he might be interested in a technique that has helped many other caring people to become more fearless, more energized, more accessible to their loved ones, and less shut down during a health crisis.

Don was skeptical at first about trying something that had spiritual or religious overtones. He'd been raised in a mostly secular family where they attended twice-a-year High Holiday services. But Don also admitted, "I've always been a little bit curious about why some people seem to feel stronger and more able to cope as a result of using prayer or meditation. I've thought of giving it a try, but the 'prove it' engineering part of me is hesitant to go in that direction."

I told Don, "I'll respect whatever you want. We can try something else if you prefer."

But a week later, Don came into our counseling session and told me, "I've sort of hit a rock bottom. I can't relax or quiet the worried thoughts in my brain about Jonah and his cancer. I can't fall back to sleep when I wake up most nights at two or three a.m. My wife and my kids say I'm cranky and uncommunicative when we're at the dinner table or driving in the car. Even my son Jonah has commented, 'Dad, where the hell are you? You used to be able to make me laugh or show me a big picture perspective that could help me deal with my problems. I want that Dad back. I miss him and I need him right now.'"

Don looked at me with a worried expression and said, "Do you think this technique for letting go of fear might work for a skeptic like me?"

I saw the fear and tension in Don's face. Since I am the parent of a son with special needs and I often walk the fine line between "wanting to be helpful to my son" and "knowing there are things I cannot change about my son's situation," I felt a strong tug at my heart. I wish I could say to Don, "It will all turn out fine," yet that would be dishonest. Instead, what I could genuinely offer him is a way to stay compassionate, energized, and more fully alive with his family as they went through this medical minefield together.

So I said to Don, "You're probably justified in having a cautious engineer's skepticism, especially when there is so much at stake. The only way to prove whether this particular tool will work for you is to do an experiment and see what happens when you try it out a few times."

For the next several weeks, Don began to say to himself a few times each morning and evening the words of Rabbi Nachman, "All the world is a very narrow bridge, and the main thing is not to fear at all."

Here's what he found from experimenting with this phrase during some painful and worrisome moments taking Jonah to chemotherapy appointments and unwinding at night after a day of inconclusive or frustrating news from the doctors. According to Don, "The first time I said the phrase I felt almost nothing. I guess I'm a bit numb or checked out from all we've been going through lately."

Don continued, "But then one night when I was up at 3:30 unable to fall back to sleep, I said the words slowly and I breathed deeply in and out. For a brief moment, I imagined a place inside myself where there is no fear, no expectations, and no pressure to make anything a certain way. Just a place where there is a lot of love for my son and my family, a lot of core strength and appreciation for this intense journey we are on. I felt a strange peacefulness that this whole cancer experience with Jonah was part of something much bigger and more mysterious than I will ever fully understand."

As Don described to me, "At that moment of just letting this world be a mystery and a narrow bridge that I definitely needed to walk across, I felt myself to be a lot less anxious and frozen. I just felt a sense of limitless love for Jonah and my family. And I listened to my breathing for a few minutes before drifting off to sleep. The next day I was a lot more alert and much less fearful. I can't quite explain what happened exactly. But seeing this whole medical challenge as a one-step-at-a-time walk across a narrow bridge helped me to focus much better when I'm with my wife and my kids. It's also freed me up to be more playful and alive both at home and at work."

The change in Don's perspective quickly became noticeable to others. Don's son Jonah commented a few weeks later to Don's wife Emily, "I think Dad is back. I was worried that this cancer thing was going to twist him up into knots permanently, but he's definitely back."

It's been several months since Don began meditating a couple times each day or night on the phrase, "The world is a very narrow bridge and the main thing is not to fear at all." According to Don, "We are still not sure if Jonah is going to recover or if we are on a sad road to losing him. But no matter what happens medically, something is different now in our family. We're closer than ever before. We're really there for each other and making each day as sweet and enjoyable as it can be. My wife Emily said to me last night, 'Don, you have become one amazing fearless leader for this family. Your eyes, your hands, your humor, your good ideas—they are keeping the rest of us strong and focused.' Then my wife put her arms around me and whispered, 'I don't know exactly what you did that made you shift from Mr. Frozen to the warm, loving, wise person you are these past few weeks. But I'm glad you did it.'"

Possibility #2:   Using the Quote as a Gentle Guide for Making Gradual Progress

For many individuals, finding a fearless place deep inside yourself isn't easy or automatic.   The rapidly pumping adrenal glands, the anxious thoughts, and the sense of danger are sometimes stronger than our ability to walk fearlessly across life's narrow bridges. Especially if you were innocently born with a highly-anxious nervous system or if you were exposed suddenly to traumatic situations in your past, there might not be an easy or quick way to shut off all the noise in your brain and achieve a state of "complete fearlessness" when an upsetting situation arises for you or your loved ones.

That's why I often recommend to people a second and equally valid way of interpreting the Rabbi Nachman phrase, "All the world is a very narrow bridge and the main thing is not to fear." You will notice the words "at all" have been removed in this second version.   That's because the word "k'lal" (like many other words in Hebrew) has more than one definition.   The final few words in Rabbi Nachman's powerful meditation phrase, "Lo l'fached k'lal" can mean "not to fear at all" or it can also mean "not to be wholly in fear" or "not to fear entirely" or "not to be completely afraid."

In other words, you can make important steps toward reducing your fear, being less anxious, or being more focused and energized as you walk carefully across one of life's narrow bridges, even if there are some lingering concerns and hesitation in the back of your mind.   Or in the words of a Los Angeles psychotherapist named Dr. Susan Jeffers, whom I met a few times several years ago, "Feel the fear and go forward anyway."

This second possibility, which allows you to be human and complex rather than fearless and one-dimensional, has proven to be a breakthrough for many of the individuals I have counseled. Here's how it works:

- **Admitting at first that you have legitimate fears and questions.** Instead of suppressing or denying the fact that you are a bit stunned to be standing on a narrow bridge with dangers all around you, how about if you just pour out your heart to a supportive listener, to God, or to yourself, saying in your own words something like, "I'm very concerned about x, y and z. I will need help to make sure I don't get frozen because of too much fear."

  Quite often the simple act of releasing or verbalizing something upsetting that has been eating away at you but is now out into the open will cause it to have less power to shut you down. A courageous person who admits, "I have a few worries and concerns…I need help to stay positive," is still a courageous person capable of walking boldly across a narrow bridge. Rabbi Nachman taught and practiced in his own life that it is healthy and energizing to take a few moments each day to "pour out your heart" to the Divine Presence. He advised people not to hold back during moments of calling out to the One who is beyond human limitations, and not to let your fears eat away at you day after day. Instead, he urged his students and followers that the more honest and real you are in your conversations with the Source of Life, the more your heartfelt spiritual relationship will give you strength and deeper wisdom.

- **Feeling the support from internal and external sources.** Once you admit to God or to a supportive ally that you have concerns and questions, now it's time to bring to mind the strengths and supports that you can count on during these next few steps along the narrow bridge. First there are the internal resources you can count on—how about your passion for moving forward, your deeply felt commitment to not staying stuck or frozen, your hard-earned training and experience that makes you more capable today of accomplishing this than you were in the past. Take a moment to ask yourself what internal strengths and experiences can you bring into this current situation to help you move forward gracefully and courageously.

Then there are the external supports—the people who have walked this path before you, the people who have given you insights and tools for making the journey safely, the people who are rooting for you, and the people who are depending on you to keep going forward. When you feel the fear causing your heart to pound or your thoughts begin racing, take a deep calming breath in and out a few times as you bring to mind the people (past and present) who are wanting you to be successful at this challenging moment.

In addition (depending on your beliefs and ideas) there might also be mysterious forces and energies that are with you and offering you strength at this moment when you are journeying forward through a narrow place of fear. For example, your connection to a loving Source, or your connection to ancestors, teachers, or role models who were courageous in situations like this in the past. Take a moment to feel your unbreakable connection to the most positive individuals in your life (past or present), that you can remember these individuals saying to you, "Don't give up. Keep going. You can do this." Even if you feel somewhat fearful and alone right now, you are not really alone if you bring these supportive energies into your awareness as you proceed forward.

- **Realizing the natural rhythms that also are directing you forward.** There are additional factors working in your favor. Rather than focusing only on what could go wrong, why not align yourself with the realities of what can go extremely well? For example, if you are in a kayak paddling through intense rapids (as my wife and I have done several times), it's crucial to do a few important things—notice the natural rhythms of the water as you lean your kayak, your body, and your mental focus forward in the direction of how the river is flowing. Then, as a second step, make sure to breathe and channel your adrenalin into a strong effort aligned with the river's energy as you keep paddling decisively (in other words, let the natural rhythms work in your favor rather than fighting them). Or, in the words of the kayak trip leader who guided us, "Hey, don't freak out. Just face downstream and keep paddling!"

In a medical situation you might be unaware of the fact the body has many built-in natural propensities to heal, to renew, to repair, plus the fact that the doctors, nurses, technicians, and aides have spent years training and preparing so that they could do a great job in your particular situation. Instead of dwelling on some medical horror story you saw on the Internet, why not focus on all the good souls and trained professionals who are doing all they can to make sure you stay safe, protected, and healthy.

Or if your narrow bridge is about a friendship, a relationship, or a work situation that has hit a bad patch, please be aware that there are natural energies in both you and the other person that are drawn toward healing, connection, love, and finding a way to renew the satisfying moments of connection you once enjoyed together. Instead of resenting or demonizing the other person, why not visualize the two of you feeling safe and at your best with each other. There are no guarantees, but if you align yourself with the possibility of things going well and you are willing to own up to your half of the problem, then the likelihood of a repair or a healing will be greatly increased.

• **Using your sense of humor to help you feel less frozen.** Finally, there is one more aspect of "not to be completely afraid" that I've found helps people enormously—namely to use your sense of humor. For example, if you can say to yourself during an anxious moment, "Thank goodness I'm not 100% terrified, I'm only 90% terrified," it can snap you out of a rigid or frozen state of mind and this kind of ironic humor then allows you to start noticing and building upon the 10% of you that is feeling competent or strong in going forward.

Or you might say to yourself, "I may be somewhat fearful and agitated right now, but there's at least an inch on my pinky finger where I'm not feeling any fear whatsoever." Just a few seconds of ironic or playful humor like this can switch your brain from feeling overwhelmed and powerless to feeling alert, creative and resourceful once again. Humor has been shown by numerous psychological researchers to have a surprisingly strong ability to re-awaken the creative, confident, and balanced part of the brain. Instead of feeling stuck or frozen as if you are permanently 100% afraid, you can use a moment of humor to say essentially, "Hey, I've got good news. I'm only 90% or 60% terrified. There is at least 10% or 40% of my brain that is still open to good ideas for moving forward safely and intelligently."

Essentially you are saying to yourself, "I've still got an unstoppable sense of humor that can poke a hole in the web of worries that was starting to shut me down." Even if a part of you remains somewhat afraid, all it takes is a part of you that is sassy, ironic, or defiantly witty to help you begin to get your strength and energy back.

The Woman Who Remembered to Use Her Sense of Humor

Charlotte's dilemma is a good example of how to deal with an intensely fearful brain (that can't be completely silenced) and yet she was willing to explore the benefits of not being "entirely afraid" or not being "wholly afraid." A creative and witty individual, Charlotte is a graphic designer who is divorced and raising two children extremely well but mostly on her own.

However, like many men and women, Charlotte was born with a genetic propensity for anxiety attacks that began to impact her life when she became a teenager. Charlotte's mom had severe anxiety attacks that limited her in many ways. Charlotte's grand-mother also had anxiety attacks in which her heart would race and it sometimes felt like she was having a heart attack, especially in certain unstructured situations.

Like many people who are genetically prone to anxiety attacks or who were raised by one or more parents who weren't very adept at mood management, Charlotte grew up thinking that each time her heart started racing with fear it meant "she might be going off the deep end." As Charlotte described, "For many years as soon as my anxiety attacks would start, I felt like a trapped passenger on an out-of-control speeding train. As a teenager and in my early 20's, there was nothing I could do to calm myself down once my heart started racing. Then a few years later I began to have side-effects from some of the pills I was given by doctors to deal with the situation."

One of Charlotte's anxiety attack triggers was the fear of giving speeches or presentations before groups of people. This was an especially important problem for her in her adult life because the success of her graphic design business and the well-being of her family depended on whether or not she could stay balanced and professional at a pitch meeting to land an assignment or at a feed-back meeting in which a group of people from her client's com-pany would evaluate and request changes in one of her designs.

That fear of having her heart race and her brain shut down dur-ing an important presentation was the reason why Charlotte came in for counseling. She had been given many different techniques and approaches over the years to "act fearless," or to "imagine the clients naked," or to "snap a rubber band on her wrist," or to "act as if...." But none of these traditional approaches worked for her. Essentially, Charlotte was not able to quiet her brain enough or to demand that it stop all fearful thoughts. Her noisy brain and her racing heart seemed to get more problematic the more she tried to shut them off.

So after several weeks of Charlotte teaching me about her lifelong experiences with anxiety attacks and the approaches that hadn't worked sufficiently thus far, I explored with her the "Possibility #2" from Rabbi Nachman's meditation phrase for allowing a moderate amount of brain noise but focusing instead on the fact that she was not "wholly afraid," "completely afraid" or "entirely afraid."

I asked Charlotte, "What if we stopped trying to turn you into someone you are not—a person who can have complete fearlessness with absolutely no noise in your brain and no racing heartbeats? What if we worked creatively with who you are genetically and experientially—someone with a very active mind and a lot of pumping in your adrenal glands?"

Charlotte smiled and replied, "I think it might be easier to work with what I've been given genetically than to twist me into a pretzel or set me up for failure trying to pretend I'm someone else."

For the next several weeks, whenever Charlotte would start anticipating a challenging situation such as an important presentation to a group of client decision-makers, she would say to herself, "All the world is a very narrow bridge, and the main thing is not to be entirely afraid," which brought a smile to her face as she realized, "Wow, I'm not completely afraid. There's a part of me that is not entirely fearful and I'm going to start building on that part of who I am."

Instead of feeling like a failure (by thinking "I must force my anxious brain to be completely quiet and I'm a failure if I'm unable to accomplish this"), she was now able to feel like a success (by reminding herself "Yes it's a fearful situation, yes I'm having some noise in my brain and some rapid heartbeats, but you know what— I'm still in the game and I'm still my creative and energetic self because I'm not entirely afraid…there are at least a few inches on my pinky finger and possibly my sexy ankle where I'm not afraid").

You will notice that this humorous and gentle method of locating the parts of your body and mind that are not afraid at the current moment is a playful and creative way of shifting your focus from dread ("Oh no, my brain is noisy and my heart is starting to beat too fast…I'm out of control") and instead focusing on what's still going right and working in your favor ("Oh yes, I'm still in charge here. I can make a joke about how my pinky finger and my sexy ankle are not feeling much fear at the moment. Since I'm not 100% anxious and I've still got my sense of defiant humor, I might as well enjoy the fact that the 10% or 40% of me that is still flowing creatively is probably going to be enough to get the job done here.")

In addition, Charlotte gave herself some internal and external reminders of support that kept her feeling strong and competent even though her brain was a bit noisy and her heartbeat was somewhat rapid. For example, she reminded herself, "I have a sizeable list of clients who have loved my design work and I've handled assignments much tougher than this one."

Charlotte also began to pray or meditate for a few minutes each morning and afternoon to lessen her fears. During one of these brief meditations, Charlotte began to breathe calmly and gently as she told herself, "I am grateful to be connected to a mysterious creative flow that I can share with clients who are seeking solutions for their design projects. I don't fully understand how this awesome creative flow works, but it seems limitless and unending, especially when I take a few moments each day to pray or meditate."

Finally, on the day of one of her presentations in front of a dozen high-powered executives, Charlotte also tapped into the natural factors that were in her favor.   She commented to herself, "These people look scary at first but at a deeper level they clearly want me to succeed and to help them come up with something that will boost their success.   That's why they invited me to show up at their conference room and to offer them some workable options.   They are going to give me edits and questions and comments not because they want to make me squirm, but because they want this to go extremely well.   Especially the woman who hired me for this project and talked about my previous good designs to her colleagues. She definitely is rooting for me to succeed.   This isn't about my fragile ego or my noisy fears—this is about being of service to some people who truly want me to do well here."

Those words of internal and external support helped Charlotte do an excellent job of presenting her new ideas to this group of high-powered executives. According to Charlotte, "I was somewhat anxious but quite alert and very alive as I walked them through various options and worked with them to improve on the specific designs they eventually selected.   Despite the fact that my heart was racing at times, it was a fantastic creative presentation and now they want me to do some other projects with them."

I have found this method of "noticing the fears inside your brain and then using your tools and support systems to go forward anyway" works often but not 100% of the time with people who have severe or moderate anxiety attacks.   Some people still need medications or additional therapies in order to balance out the chemistry that is racing at moments like these.

But if you are someone who was born with a lot of anxious propensities or if you have become more anxious during your lifetime because of traumatic, upsetting or disappointing things that have happened to you, please give this second possibility of reducing the intensity of your fears a solid chance to succeed.

Seeing the Narrow Bridges from a Different Perspective

Finally, if you want to benefit from Rabbi Nachman's famous quote to lift yourself or someone else out of excessive fear or agitation, there is one more important and useful aspect to consider: Ask yourself, "What do you think it means when the beginning of Rabbi Nachman's famous quote says, 'All the world is a very narrow bridge...'"

There are several possible interpretations of this well-known opening phrase. Here are three widely-accepted ways of understanding these profound words for seeing in a new light the pressures and challenges you face. Please take a moment to consider whether one or more of these brief teachings about "All the world is a very narrow bridge" might possibly be strengthening and comforting for you during an anxious moment now or in the future:

Interpretation A: Maybe the very narrow bridge is referring to the idea that your soul is more enduring and expansive than this narrow lifetime. There's a wonderful teacher in Los Angeles named Olivia Schwartz whom I've studied with several times. She is extremely knowledgeable about Jewish mysticism and Chasidic spiritual practices. She interprets the "very narrow bridge" as a description of just how confining and limited it is for our expansive soul to have to enter a time-limited and kvetchy human body. Olivia Schwartz often says, "An immortal soul trying to function in a constricted body is like putting on a pair of shoes that are two sizes too small. You can do it, barely, but it's extremely confining and sometimes painful."

In other words, she is saying, "Look at this temporary situation, this narrow bridge, as if you are an immortal soul with many lifetimes to figure things out." While the majority of 21st century

Jews have been taught by their parents or their friends that "Jews don't believe in an after-life," in fact there have been fascinating theories and ideas for over 3,000 years from Jewish writings and teachings about various possibilities of what it means for an immortal soul to enter a confined human body for a brief time period of 100 years or less in order to learn lessons, do good deeds, and help repair the world.

Almost 20 years ago I read an excellent book called "Jewish Views of the Afterlife" by Jewish psychologist and pastoral counselor Simcha Paull Raphael. He describes in detail how Jewish writers, teachers, mystics and scholars in various time periods (the Biblical writings, the Rabbinic writings, the Medieval authors, the Kabbalists, and the 20th century writers) have envisioned the process of the soul entering and leaving the body.

I find it frequently intriguing and sometimes comforting to explore the many ideas and possibilities of how our amazing souls need to inhabit a body and a personality in order to do some important work on Earth and how the soul quite possibly continues to live on after our bodies have stopped breathing.

The author Simcha Paull Raphael doesn't twist your arm or ask you to believe anything that doesn't make sense to you. In fact, you don't need to read his entire book to get a healthy sampling of the many creative and inspiring visions there are of the ways that Judaism offers for transcending the painful limitations of being mortal and vulnerable. Raphael gently lays out numerous possibilities to consider and then you can decide for yourself which ideas feel reasonable and which theories feel ridiculous.

In the years since Raphael wrote his ground-breaking book, there have been numerous other books, courses, and teachings on how to understand the Jewish possibilities for envisioning your soul being part of something bigger and more enduring than the problems of the moment. If you have ever felt a desire to understand the concept of "what is my soul's journey" or "what might be my soul's higher purpose," please make sure to give yourself the opportunity to study more and learn more about this crucial topic.

Even if you can't prove scientifically that you have an immortal soul or that your soul is far more expansive than the constricted mortal body that currently houses your exquisite soul, it still might open up your imagination and your energy to see yourself as part of an endless flow of creation. During a stressful moment on a narrow bridge, you can feel a lot more curious, compassionate and calm when you sense this current challenge is part of an ongoing process that is being sorted out over more than just one lifetime.

Interpretation B: The idea of a "very narrow bridge" might be referring to the fact that we often require some tense struggles and narrow passages in order to focus, learn, grow, and develop to higher levels of awareness. In 12-step programs (for food, alcohol, drugs, gambling, co-dependency, or other addictions) you often find that well-intentioned people frequently don't change a long-time habit until they lose something precious or they hit a rock bottom in which the old coping strategies simply don't work any longer. Or in your own life, have you ever noticed that sometimes it takes a crisis, a major loss, or an intense moment of frustration before you are motivated enough to try something new or deepen your search for truth?

It's similar to the Chinese language where the word for "crisis" has two characters, one representing "precarious trial" or "danger," while the other character in the word "crisis" means "opportunity" or "critical point."

So when Rabbi Nachman says, "The whole world is a very narrow bridge," he might be urging us to see each challenge, frustration, or constriction as a gift or an opportunity that wakes us up to pay attention, learn, grow, and connect with a more expansive perspective. This is not always easy or automatic, but he's saying that if you make sure not to fall into fear or frozenness, you will be energized by the narrow precarious bridge to pay close attention and do your very best to proceed forward wisely.

To see if this second interpretation rings true for you or someone you know, ask yourself, "Have I ever been sluggish or inconsistent in pursuing something important, but only when it became a very intense narrow bridge with severe consequences and time pressures did I wake up sufficiently to do a much more effective job of moving forward? Did it take a feeling of crisis or precariousness to inspire me (or someone else) to give it a higher priority and to do a much better job?

Interpretation C: The narrow bridge may seem overwhelming at first, but Rabbi Nachman teaches that joy, gratitude and compassion can be excellent companions on the journey across a narrow bridge. If you are going on a complicated journey, especially a journey through treacherous wild waters, dark forests, or intense challenges, what would you like to take with you as your traveling companions?

You could bring huge batches of fear along and spend each moment of the journey hearing in your head a litany of anxious thoughts and worst-case-scenarios. Or you can take along a specific toolbox (let's call it the Rabbi Nachman Assortment) of things for which are you are grateful, experiences that give you joy, prayers that keep your heart open, and consistent calm breathing that connects you with the flow of the universe.

You get to decide what you will bring on your journey today, this week, and this year. Will your body and mind be subjected to nothing but fear and tightness, or will they be receiving reminders of joy, compassion, gratitude, and oxygen so you can begin to glimpse beyond the narrow places to the possibilities for healing and renewal that await you on the other side of the narrow bridge?

Please don't feel like a failure if there is still a moderate amount of noise or anxiety in your brain. All of us will continue to have occasional rushes of fear or adrenalin, even if you are just inches away from being an enlightened master.   But if you make a conscious effort as you approach a narrow bridge to recall at least one thing of joy, one feeling of gratitude, and one reason for being compassionate and strong, you probably will outsmart the anxious part of your brain and reconnect with the resilient, courageous, and energized parts of who you are.

I often say to counseling clients and to myself: "When you start to feel challenged or overloaded by what you are facing, that's a moment to breathe calmly and decide which will it be for you—an endless flood of anxious thoughts or a welcome relief of supportive, nourishing thoughts."   I'll let you decide.

CHAPTER 5

TREATING YOUR BODY WITH GREATER
UNDERSTANDING AND CARE

I magine that you were asked to be the caretaker for a valuable but quite fragile and breakable gift that contains some of the holiest sparks in the universe.

The gift I am talking about is your body, your physical self during this lifetime. The holy sparks are the creative ideas, the loving energies, the beautiful movements, the subtle wisdom, the Divine inputs, and the built-in potentials for healing, growth, aging, and renewal that are contained in every cell of your body.

In Jewish writings and teachings for thousands of years, the responsibility to be an excellent, loving caretaker for your body is described as one of the most important parts of being alive. From the first breath to the final breath, the chance to be the shomeir (the trustworthy and compassionate protector) of the fragile vessel that contains your soul is considered an awesome opportunity.

But underneath these flowery words about taking good care of your body, let's be real about this. What exactly is your personal feeling about your body and your physical self:

- Does it seem exciting and energizing to know you are the caretaker of something so holy, delicate, and constantly changing?
- Or is it daunting and challenging to be asked to take good care of something so fragile, complicated, and breakable?
- Or do you tend to fluctuate between wanting to be a good caretaker for your physical self but often you are feeling burdened, bothered, or oblivious to the task?
- Or do you find yourself resenting that the particular body you were given is not as beautiful, healthy, resilient, or co-operative as some of the other bodies you've noticed?

This chapter is about discovering a deep and profound Jewish perspective that can dramatically change and improve how you deal with your physical self. Whether you are a strong believer, a somewhat skeptical person, or someone who has intermittent moments of belief and moments of doubt, you probably will be surprised at how these Jewish teachings about the body can inspire you to become a far more adept and successful caretaker for the amazingly complex systems that are involved in your physical well-being. Even if you have struggled in the past with your weight, your physical agility, your health, your vitality, or your personal self-worth because of the body you were given, this chapter possibly will open you up to a new way of making peace between your spirit, your mind, and your body.

Identifying the Urge to Not Listen to the Body's Signals

Before we get to the breakthrough insights that come from Jewish teachings, I need to ask you to do a short quiz that will identify what's at issue here and how much you may have gotten sidetracked from the holy task of being a consistently excellent caregiver for your physical self. As one of my favorite teachers, Rabbi Ted Falcon of Seattle, Washington, likes to say, "Since we are human, we are the ones who frequently forget our holy purposes in life. But sometimes we remember to remember them."

Here's a brief list of questions that you can answer on your own or with a supportive friend or family member to see the extent to which you have sometimes forgotten to take good care of the body that has been gifted to you. Please be honest:

- Do you sometimes feel as if you are barely keeping up with the demands of daily living and you haven't had the time or energy to check in very often with what your body is telling you about what it needs, what it doesn't need, or how it's doing moment to moment?
- Or when you do notice an early-warning signal from your muscles, your nerves, your tendons, or your internal organs, do you ever feel too over-scheduled or too busy to deal with what your body is needing or asking from you?
- Do you sometimes baby your body too much or fail to bring out its best potential?
- Do you sometimes resent or feel frustrated that you have a body that needs special care or that has specific limits, challenges, and vulnerabilities?
- Do you sometimes do the opposite of what your body needs because you are magically hoping that you can get away with doing what others seem to get away with?
- Do you ever talk to your vulnerable physical self with a harsh, angry, or dismissive tone in the hope that your body will either comply or that it might miraculously change and not require specific considerations and limits?

If you answered "Yes" to one or more of the above questions, please consider yourself to be in good company. We all have moments when we run away from the awesome responsibility of taking excellent care of this complicated physical self that we have been given by a mysterious Source. Fortunately, you are also honest enough and conscious enough to begin the process of seeking peace between the part of you that knows a lot about how to be an excellent personal caregiver and the part of you that tends to forget or reject this huge responsibility.

Is it possible to change or improve your partnership with the complicated and vulnerable body that houses your pure soul? That's what we're going to explore in the next several pages. For a start, here is a quick illustration of a highly-intelligent person who wished she didn't have so many challenging body issues to take into account each day. See if her story sounds like your own story or that of someone you know:

The Talented Woman Who Trained for the Top
Arianna is a hard-working physician in her late 30's who has often been a high achiever. For instance, in middle school she won awards for competitive gymnastics and in college she was near the top of her class with a double major in Biology and Post-Modern Literature.

As Arianna explained to me during one of her counseling sessions, "I need to do something about my health challenges. I used to be able to get away with pushing my body and not worrying about the consequences. But lately I'm not as invincible as I wish I could be."

When we began to explore further how Arianna felt about her physical self, she admitted, "I seem to have learned in gymnastics training to ignore the pain signals my body was sending me. I won awards and got a lot of applause because I was able to keep pushing my body to do vaults, leaps, flips, and poses that were beyond what a normal human being could do. Of course I paid the price and I eventually had to deal with muscle aches, bone chips, spinal issues, some nerve damage, headaches, and lots of torn ligaments and tissues that never fully healed from all those years as a competitive gymnast. But I sure loved the trophies and the exhilaration."

In addition, during her training to become a physician, Arianna realized, "I had gotten quite familiar with how to disregard the things my body was telling me about lack of sleep, rushed meals, long shifts, and grueling schedules." She admits, "It was somewhat of a competitive pride thing. The docs who could suck it up, drink a lot of caffeine, and never say no to an unreasonable demand were the ones we all looked to as heroes. No one wanted to admit that we might be human or vulnerable."

Now at the age of 38, Arianna is starting to rethink her ideas about her health and well-being. She's had trouble getting pregnant, she's also dealing with a serious case of adult-onset diabetes, and she's recently discovered that her feet, her ankles, and her spine might need additional surgeries to correct some of the damage from her years as an award-winning gymnast.

Does her story sound like what you or a loved one have gone through? Has a genetic propensity (like diabetes) or a long-time pursuit of something important (like the sleep deprivation of certain stressful careers or unrelenting family responsibilities) caused your physical self to become more prone to illness and less able to bounce back quickly? Have you tended to put extra stress on your body because you thought you could somehow get away with it year after year?

What Arianna explored with me in counseling is the question most people face at some point in their 30's, 40's, 50's, 60's, 70's or 80's. Specifically, she looked me in the eye during one of our sessions and asked, "Why am I so unwilling to do the sensible things my body seems to need? Why am I still acting like a defiant teenager who thinks she can just cheat or ignore what I've been advised to do about food, sleep, exercise, blood sugar monitoring, and other forms of self-care? I wish I didn't have to deal with these physical-care issues. But sometimes I wonder what it's going

to take before I start giving excellent care to this increasingly delicate and complex body I have…a challenged body that is no longer
keeping up with the pressures I put on it."

Connecting with a Powerful Sacred Approach to Caring for Your Body

Since Arianna was part-Jewish and had recently become somewhat
interested in various alternative methods of healing, I asked her if she
might be open to learning a very simple but profound tool that has
been explored in Jewish teachings and writings for many centuries.

Arianna thought for a moment and then replied, "I'd like to
learn something new and different from the repetitive pill-popping
and surgeries I was trained to do in medical school. But is this
'Jewish spiritual approach' like some sort of faith healing where a
person relies only on prayer and belief instead of medicine?"

I answered, "No, it's not an either/or situation where you'd have
to choose between medical wisdom and spiritual wisdom. In fact,
these Jewish methods are quite compatible with whatever current
medicine or alternative healing methods you prefer. In Judaism,
there is no separation or battle between the latest medical science,
or the latest non-traditional holistic approaches, and the spiritual
aspects of healing. Maimonides and many other revered Jewish
spiritual teachers were also physicians and healers who were constantly learning from the latest advances of their era. The approach in Judaism is to draw from all useful possibilities to combine
the wisdom of the mind, the wisdom of the body, and the wisdom
of the spirit in an integrated way that treats you as a whole person
in a world that has numerous healing possibilities and resources."

Arianna smiled and commented, "Do you mean I can do something a little bit 'out there and spiritual' without losing my cred-
ibility as a scientist?"

I laughed and said, "Absolutely. In Judaism you can tap
into both the scientific part of your brain and the curious, holy,

transcendent part of your brain. If we're hoping to improve your health and your aliveness, why not go all out and draw from several different helpful and profound sources?"

The Words and Actions That Might Stir Up Improved Results
So we began to discuss and test out the ancient Jewish words of healing and physical care that have been spoken, meditated, and studied for thousands of years. Specifically, I asked Arianna to start practicing a few minutes each day by breathing deeply, closing her eyes, and saying three simple but profound meditation phrases that come from Jewish prayers and healing methods. The three phrases are:

Re-fu-aht Ha-Nef-esh ("Heal or renew the spirit")
Re-fu-aht Ha-Guf ("Heal or renew the body")
Re-fu-ah Sh'lay-ma (which can be translated in several ways, including "Help me to feel whole and complete again" or "Restore me to wholeness and completeness")

In order to attain the full value and impact of these three phrases, it's important to know what they mean in both spiritual and practical terms. Then when you say them to boost your own health or the health of someone you are caring for, your words and your intentions will go much deeper than if you just say them without much awareness.

Part One: What Does It Really Mean to Say "Heal or Renew the Spirit"?
Like most people, Arianna wondered why the Jewish prayers for healing start with the statement to "Heal or Renew the Spirit." Why not go directly to a request to heal the body? Why start with the spirit?

Like a flame that needs wind to grow stronger, the quest for healing and renewal needs a lot of energy from the soul, the spirit, or the flow of the universe in order to be effective. It's much harder to heal or improve some vulnerable aspect of your physical self if you are feeling shut down, exhausted, or consumed by discouragement and uncertainty.

The words are easy to remember: Re-fu-aht (heal or renew) Ha-Nefesh (the spirit or soul that is within me). In essence, this meditation phrase is saying, "Open up a channel of healing energy and flow that is currently closed. Open up my awareness so that I can see what might be the next productive steps I can take on this journey of self-care. Open up my connection to the light, the strength, or the caring that is available to me if I am willing to reach out for it and receive it. Open up my connection to the infinite Source that is continually creating, repairing, and inspiring. Don't let me close myself off from what is possible from the loving and supportive people who want to boost my spirits so that I might be able to heal or improve."

(If these words are more spiritual or religious than you are comfortable with, please put in your own words about opening up your spirit and reconnecting with the flow of healing that is within you and around you. There isn't one rigid way to say these words, especially since they are about tapping into the hard-to-define energies of your own unique transcendent spirit).

Since Arianna was trained as a scientist and a physician, she was naturally a bit skeptical at first about whether she could connect her tired spirit with the impossible-to-quantify Spirit of the Universe. That's true for many people. When your body is aching and the remedies aren't quite bringing sufficient relief, it's not easy to take a breath and say, "Please open up my spirit to the healing flow of energy and caring from a Source I cannot fully define."

So I asked Arianna to consider each time she meditated on the phrase "Re-fu-aht Ha-Nefesh, Heal or renew my spirit," the following questions:

- What do you personally envision the words "Heal the spirit" or "Renew the spirit" could mean for your particular situation?

- What would it be like if your soul or your spirit were flourishing strongly even if your body was still facing some serious challenges?
- How might a renewed spirit or a healed spirit help you open up to new ideas, new approaches, new support, and new energy for addressing your physical situation?
- How might a renewed spirit or a healed spirit give you additional strength, endurance, and resilience to go through all the challenging steps you will need to go through on this journey of improved care?

In other words, when you say silently or out loud, "Re-fu-aht Ha-Nefesh, heal or renew the spirit," you are not just calling out to God to offer crucial assistance, guidance and strength. You are also calling out to yourself to awaken your soul and your spirit to the healing possibilities and flexibility you might have closed off as a result of several disappointments or setbacks. Whether you are dealing with an acute ailment or a long-term chronic condition, taking a moment to stir up a sense of renewed spirit will give you much more ko-ach (the Hebrew word for strength) to stay on track and not shut down for too long through all the ups and downs of attending to your complicated health situation.

Part Two: What Happens When You Meditate on the Words "Heal or Renew the Body."
In this second phrase, the ancient words of healing focus directly on the physical issues for which you are seeking improvement and relief. If you breathe gently, close your eyes, and say the middle phrase with deep intention, "Re-fu-aht Ha-Guf, Heal or renew the body," you can tap into some important perspectives about how to help the healing process within your body.

For instance, even if there is still a genetic propensity within you to have certain physical challenges, you are taking a moment to envision the best possible situation (given those genetic challenges).   I know this from personal experience because I have a genetic condition called Celiac Disease that requires me to avoid certain foods (in my case it's dairy, wheat, corn and sugar) that can cause two to seven days of pain and problems.   When I breathe deeply, close my eyes, and say, "Re-fu-aht Ha-Guf, heal or renew my body," I don't expect to change the genetic situation, but I am grateful for how much that meditation phrase helps me stay centered and on track for doing what my body needs and, as a result, being quite healthy and productive most of the time.

Or if you have experienced something jarring during your time on Earth that has injured or severely impacted some aspect of your physical self, then by saying the words, "Re-fu-aht Ha-Guf, Heal or renew the body," you are envisioning the best available improvement (given the ongoing realities of your injury).   You probably can't go back to the same body you had before the serious injury, but you can improve how your body functions and how excellent your life can be even with the after-effects of that injury.

Or if your body has, for reasons that might never be clear, developed an ailment or a long-term condition that is challenging, these words ("Heal or renew the body") can open up your mind and spirit to consider "What is the next positive step on this path of self-care and maximizing my potential?   What am I possibly doing that is making the situation stagnant or worse? What kind of support and guidance will I need to take this next positive step forward?" Even if the medical condition continues to be part of your life for a long time, you can still use this meditation phrase to focus on how to maximize what your body can still do and how full your life can be.

As I explained to Arianna, "Prayer and meditation are not about barking a rigid ultimatum to God or the universe, 'Either fix this physical problem 100% right now or I will stop believing in

You altogether.' Rather, the moments of breathing, praying, and meditating are about expanding your awareness and opening you up to possibilities for connecting more fully to the care and wisdom that is available to you if you get beyond your anxieties, your discouragement, and your hesitations. Prayer and meditation are about opening up a partnership between you and the One that surrounds you with helpful possibilities. Or opening up a partnership between you and all the expertise, lovingkindness, and creative solutions that you might not have felt fully ready to take into your fragile body thus far."

I suggested to Arianna that when she was meditating on the words "Heal or renew the body," she might consider these questions (that have proven helpful for many of my counseling clients and workshop participants):

- What have you learned so far about what levels of stress or pushing your body a little or a lot can cause your body's symptoms to get worse or to get better?
- What have you noticed are the foods, specific exercises, flexibility stretching, supportive treatments, water intake, and remedies that cause your particular body to start improving or worsening?
- What are the amounts of sleep, meditation, or unwinding time that your unique body prefers or desperately needs?
- What is one thing about your physical self that you haven't fully accepted or appreciated, and this personal reluctance is possibly harming your longevity or your daily aliveness?
- What role models, coaching, teamwork, and guidance can help you say yes to life and yes to the realities of your complicated physical vessel, even if the physical challenges continue to some extent or if there are setbacks?
- What are one or two positive steps you could do starting immediately for taking excellent care of your body if you

believed (even slightly) that it is a holy gift and you are the trusted protector of that gift even during frustrating moments?

This spiritual idea of "saying yes to life in all its complexities even on difficult days" and saying "yes to the realities of your particular body even when there are challenges" is very similar to a psychological teaching that has inspired me and many others. It's called "The Paradoxical Theory of Change" and it was developed by a Gestalt therapist named Arnold Beisser.

Beisser was a brilliant and energetic human being, a competitive tennis player and passionate student during his early years, who found he was unable to use his limbs after the age of 25 because of polio-related ailments. Yet despite being severely physically challenged and confined to a chair the rest of his life, he helped many thousands of people as a psychotherapist, teacher, mentor, and writer (his books include the 1989 bestseller "Flying Without Wings").

In his highly-influential 1970 article "The Paradoxical Theory of Change," Beisser explained how difficult it is to achieve one's potential or make positive changes if you are resenting or resisting what the facts are about your situation. Then he describes how much more grounded, centered, solid, energized, alive, and effective you can be if you start with a deeper understanding and appreciation of what your current physical or emotional situation entails, especially if it means accepting and appreciating your genuine limitations, struggles, and occasional setbacks.

The "Paradoxical Theory of Change" is similar to the process of driving successfully in a deep pile of snow and ice. For anyone who has ever tried to drive a car that is immersed in 10 inches of icy snow, you know that you can't just gun the motor and go forward—that will only spin your wheels. Nor can you sit there endlessly hoping the snow will melt—it might take days or weeks before there is good traction again. What works to get a car out of 10 inches of snow is the same thing that works when you are feeling stuck with a medical or physical condition—you have to consciously go forward and back, forward and back, which helps you get enough traction to suddenly notice that your tires are grabbing hold and your vehicle is moving forward smoothly. You can't criticize yourself (or your vehicle) for needing to go back a little bit several times in order to gain a foothold and then go forward with much better traction. It's the only way to get unstuck.

To paraphrase Arnold Beisser, "If you get fully clear and honest about where you are at the moment, even if it includes pain, frustration and some back-tracking, then you can go forward with increased self-awareness, compassion, strength and vitality. Being honest and honoring your moment-to-moment reality gives you traction and integrity. You are no longer at war with yourself or stuck in a self-hating spiral of shame, denial, and trying to save face. Instead, you are free to respect the reasons why you needed to stop for a moment or take a step backward, so that you can then go forward with much better care and love for how complicated and amazing it is to be a human being."

Or in Beisser's own words, "Change happens when somebody is what he is, not if he's trying to be someone he's not."

So when a person prays or meditates on the words "Heal or renew my body," or when you live according to the ideas of "The Paradoxical Theory of Change," you have an opportunity each day to become much wiser, more honest, and more caring as to what your unique body is going through, what it needs, and what it doesn't need. You are making positive changes not from a place of fantasy or impossibly false hopes, but rather from a grounded, centered, one-step-at-a-time solidness that can put you on a firmer track for getting the excellent physical care and guidance your body requires on a daily basis.

Part Three: What Does It Mean to Envision a Refuah Sh'layma or a "Return to Feeling Whole and Complete Again?"

Now we arrive at the most profound and inspiring part of the Jewish phrases for healing.   The third phrase, "Re-fu-ah sh'lay-ma" can be translated as either "A complete healing" or "A return to wholeness and completeness."

The word "refuah" means healing or renewal and the word "sh'lay-ma" is related to the word "shalom" which can mean hello, goodbye, peace, wholeness, completeness, or the Oneness and alignment of all that had seemed separate and fragmented.

As you think about your own situation (physically, emotionally, spiritually), you might find yourself fixated on one painful symptom or one less-than-ideal physical aspect of your appearance or your health.   But in the Hebrew phrase "Refuah sh'layma, help me to feel whole and complete again," there is a leap of consciousness from the narrowness of "one painful symptom" to a renewed awareness that you are "an amazing vessel that has thousands of things working well and is also connected to a universe that is truly awesome."

"Now hold on," you might be saying.   The arthritis in your neck and shoulders is screaming and this author is saying, "Get in touch with the fact that your amazing vessel has thousands of things working well and is also connected to a universe that is truly awesome."   "To heck with that," might be your first response.

But let's take a moment to breathe, close your eyes, and say calmly, "Re-fu-ah sh'lay-ma, help me to feel whole and complete again."   Is it possible (despite the pain in one part of your physical self) to connect with the fact that your mind, your body, and your spirit are functioning well in a thousand other ways.   For just a second, please mention to yourself at least three things that are going well in your body right at this moment.   Is your heart beating and do you have a pulse?   I sure hope so.   Is there some section of your body that doesn't have pain at the moment?   Great.   Breathe into that pain-free section for a moment. Is there something about your situation right now that includes a little bit of love or care from someone? Is there something that is a slight bit better today than it was yesterday or last month?

To feel whole and complete does not negate or ignore the fact that there is pain and some complicated stuff going in your body. Rather, you can rest assured that feeling whole and complete will embrace the pain, embrace the challenges, and embrace the courage that are required to live more fully each day even though there are physical pains and personal challenges asking for attention within your body and mind.

In Jewish spirituality, there doesn't need to be a war inside you. You can embrace the difficulties and breathe into the physical pain. You can celebrate the things that are going well and breathe calmly into a deep sense of gratitude and hope as well as breathing calmly into the challenges and roller coasters of your health situation.

Is that easy to do? Sometimes yes and sometimes no. The brain tends to focus on what's not going right because the brain likes to solve problems. But sometimes if you pray, meditate, breathe, or say things like "Refuah sh'layma, let me feel whole and complete again," it is not too difficult to have moments of experiencing a beautiful at-one-ment with all that is happening inside you and around you. You might even feel a sense of peace as you breathe lovingly in and out, and you silently affirm the Oneness of all that exists. From a spiritual perspective, you are not isolated and alone. You are connected to the ever-flowing life force that surrounds you and moves through your holy vessel, your body.

For a moment, see how much you can experience a feeling of wholeness and completeness regarding the beautiful soul that you are (at your core essence) and the complicated but sufficient body that has been given to you in order to house that precious soul. Ask yourself:

- When you think of your own soul and your own essence, are you able for a few moments to stop fixating on the slightly-broken vessel and instead truly connect with what's inside the vessel?

- When you try on the words "I am whole and complete," can you forgive yourself for all the judgments, expectations, criticisms and detours that have caused you to lose sight of the fact that in the big picture (or the unconditional love of the Creative Source) you are probably viewed as sufficient, whole, complete and worthy of being loved?

- When you think about your health issues and your physical challenges, can you step back for a moment and just accept the fact that human beings are not built to be flawless, but in the cracks, the vulnerabilities, and the brokenness (if we embrace them, too) we find a way to love ourselves and to love this life in all its fullness and variations.

Connecting to a Peaceful Wholeness During a Health Crisis

A few years ago I had a surprise one morning when my vision went dark in the top third of my right eye and I was told by the doctor I consulted that I needed immediate surgery for a detached retina.

I said, "What if I put off the surgery until it's convenient for my schedule." He said, "You'll go blind."

At that moment, my adrenal glands were pumping and I asked for a glass of water because as I explained, "My mouth is a bit dry and it feels very warm in here." But as soon as I began to meditate on the ancient words to "heal the spirit, heal the body, and help me feel whole and complete again," I was able to breathe calmly during the pre-surgery preparations, the post-surgical recovery, and the ten days of lying face down (with some excellent books on tape and a few music CD's) so that the surgically-repaired retina could attach well and possibly allow me to see again eventually. After two eye surgeries, I am much more conscious and caring toward my eyes than I had ever been. There is no longer a moment when I take for granted that the eyes are an amazing gift and that they are so fragile and in need of precise continual care.

What are the health crises and wake-up calls that you and your loved ones have experienced? Have you found a way to stay conscious and caring about the fragile, breakable gifts of your physical self that you have been given and what it will take to help those gifts improve and stay functional for a long time to come? Have you been able to appreciate that you are a whole person worthy of love and support, even though a part of you might be broken or challenged?

Restoring your sense of wholeness often takes time and a strong sincere intention. Over the past twenty years, I have counseled men and women who have been diagnosed with multiple sclerosis, lung problems, cancer, post-polio disorders, heart problems, digestive ailments, diabetes, Crohns, celiac, reproductive difficulties, migraines, fibromyalgia, arthritis, addictions, immune system disorders, and numerous other painful physical situations. In most cases, there was a feeling at first of "being betrayed by one's body" that needed to be explored before moving gradually to a restoration of feeling whole and complete again.

Sometimes it took weeks, months, or years to regain a sense of strength and clarity that despite the physical challenges, you are still a whole and fully alive individual who can say yes to the numerous challenges and the equally numerous joys of your daily life. In a few cases, the person who came for counseling was unable to let go of the feelings of "why me," "why can't my body do what this other person's body can do," or "I simply don't have the desire to feel whole or worthy again—I'm much too broken." Sometimes our psychological and spiritual goals do not have a 100% guarantee.

What seems to make the difference and has helped over 90% of the people with serious ailments whom I have counseled is the belief they developed sooner or later that, "We are the caretakers for something holy and amazing, this complicated body that houses our precious soul." As one counseling client explained it to me, "If I were just supposed to do positive things for my body because it's only for my selfish benefit, I might flake out a bit. But when I remember that I'm doing this as the caretaker or protector for something holy that comes from a Higher Source that relies on me and my daily efforts, then we're talking about something that I just can't ignore or avoid as easily."

Or in the words of another counseling client, "It's one thing to cheat on my food plan or my exercise plan because I'm not feeling motivated or worthy that day. But if I think it's about doing something for God and the unique gift that God has given me to be alive with a vulnerable body that I'm in charge of, then I want to do a much better job of it."

The Moment When Arianna Shifted Her Viewpoint

You probably recall earlier in the chapter how Arianna, the physician and former gymnast who was dealing with diabetes, infertility issues, athletic injuries, and recurring pain, was asking, "What's it going to take before I stop cheating or ignoring what my body needs regarding food, sleep, exercise, blood sugar monitoring, and other forms of care."

During one of our counseling sessions, I asked her the question of whether or not she had ever imagined her body to be a precious gift on loan from the Creative Source of the Universe. She laughed for a moment and said, "Look, I'm a trained doctor. I'm not supposed to get all warm and fuzzy like that."

But a week later she came into my office and admitted, "I've been up several times this week wondering how long I'm going to keep ignoring the fact that in my heart I do believe there is something incredible and mystical about the human body and how it seems connected to energy fields and intuitive wisdom that are way beyond what we were allowed to talk about in medical school. I'm not sure exactly what I believe or don't believe about God and how God functions. But I do feel a sense of awe and amazement at how the body works, how the universe works, and how much daily focus and teamwork it takes to do a great job of caring for this fragile body and the fragile planet that carry us through life."

Arianna then explained, "I woke up yesterday morning with a sense that I have been given a very important job to do in this lifetime. I need to take much better care of my breakable body and my fluctuating health. Even though I am a scientist by training and temperament, I do believe I have a soul and that this body is housing my soul for as long as I am able to take good care of it. If that means no longer cheating or ignoring the things I need to do to improve my health and find the right experts and methods to help my body thrive for a very long time, then I'm fully committed to that positive quest from now on. You might need to ask me in six months or a year if I'm still on track. But I'm a stubborn person and if I say I'm going to be a much better caregiver for this gift I've been given, I expect in six months or a year I will be mostly on track doing a fairly good job."

A year later I had a follow-up session with Arianna and I am happy to report that she is still doing quite well at being the best caregiver imaginable for her complicated and vulnerable physical self. I hope her story inspires you to do the same for the valuable and breakable gift you have been given. I believe it's a holy task to listen to one's body and treat it with wisdom and lovingkindness, so I hope you find lots of supportive people and methods to help you be extremely successful at it.

CHAPTER 6

EXPLORING INNER REPAIR AND

OUTER REPAIR

Which do you think is more important: self-improvement or repairing the world around you? If you only have a limited amount of time in a given week or a busy year, which of these two important quests is the one you would focus on the most—inner repair or outer repair?

Here's a possible answer: A number of years ago my wife Linda and I went to a "Peacemakers Gathering," a three day event for hundreds of artists, activists, health practitioners, entrepreneurs, and spiritual leaders at a rustic conference center two hours from where we live. We weren't sure what to expect, but we drove up to the main lodge and met a wide variety of individuals from diverse religions, races, backgrounds, and viewpoints.

During that intense weekend, there was a recurring argument between two different groups about what is most important in the quest for peace and repair. The individuals in one of the groups, which I will call "The Innies," were saying repeatedly that getting up early each day to meditate, stretch or exercise, work on your own self, and live more simply were the most important ways to achieve peace and improve life on Earth. Then there was a second group, which I will call "The Outies" and they were saying repeatedly that getting involved in helping others in need, or in political and environmental causes, or in local and global teamwork projects were the best ways to achieve peace and improve what can be improved.

The argument between the "Innies" and the "Outies" went on for two days and nights until on the third day a thoughtful and articulate rabbi spoke up and suggested, "In Judaism we usually say 'Choose both approaches, making sure each day to spend a few minutes in honest reflection working on some aspect of your personal issues and also making time whenever possible to do something constructive about one or more aspects of the brokenness in the world.'"

In other words, in Judaism you can be both an "Innie" and an "Outie" because there are specific prayers and steps to make sure each day, each week, and each year you find a deeper sense of purpose and meaning by taking action in two crucial areas of being fully alive:

- First, to take an honest "accounting of your soul" (in Hebrew it's called a Cheshbon Ha-nefesh) every so often in order to make some progress on a specific character trait or habit of yours that needs a bit of improvement. Many Jews review "what needs improving, what is still difficult or challenging, and what am I learning about how to be a more balanced and aligned individual" at the end of each day, or each week, or during the weeks prior to the High Holidays each year. It's not about beating yourself up, but rather about clarifying which behaviors, habits, and situations need extra work because these parts of you are not yet at the level you are capable of reaching in this lifetime.
- Second, there is also a strong emphasis in Judaism to notice and become active regarding one or more unfair,

unbalanced, or insensitive situations in the world for which you can give some time, energy, or generosity in order to move toward a tikkun olam, a repair of the world. Even if you are busy with your job, your family, or your health challenges, there is always the possibility of doing something positive to repair some aspect of the world that is broken or dysfunctional and that moves you personally.

As you think about your own life thus far, have you tended to lean in the direction of inner repair (meditation, inner peace, prayer, examining your habits and personal growth steps)? Or have you leaned in the direction of outer work (pursuing a quest to improve some aspect of your local community, or the environment, or the sense of justice and human dignity in the world around you)?

Doing Both: Will You Feel Depleted or Energized?
Now consider for a moment what would your life be like if you had the chance to make slow-but-steady progress year after year on both your personal growth and your effectiveness in repairing a corner of the world? What if you could find just enough time, energy, and support to do BOTH of these awesome things during each new year of your life?

Since most people today are already overloaded up to their eyeballs with things to do each week, the very thought of "repairing your inner self" while also "repairing the world" could sound overwhelming at first. You might be wondering, "Is there really a balanced and healthy way to seek inner repair and outer repair at the same time, or do these complicated quests tend to tip you over into unrealistic expectations, burnout, and discouragement?"

In order to be successful at both inner repair and outer repair, there are some genuine obstacles that need to be addressed. For example, ask yourself:

- Have you ever joined a group of "do-gooders" to help repair some aspect of the world, but the in-fighting, the big personalities, or the interpersonal dynamics within the group got in the way?
- Have you ever tried to improve some aspect of your own character or your way of dealing with life's challenging moments, but you were surprised to discover layers of resistance and hesitation that you hadn't known were there?
- Have you ever felt drained or discouraged by a time-consuming and complicated project to help others and as a result you felt you weren't paying sufficient time or energy to your own needs or your family's needs?
- Have you ever felt frustrated that you wanted to be part of something meaningful and profound, but you got pulled away suddenly by other demands on your time?

My goal in this chapter is to help you find the right combinations of inner work and outer involvement that feel balanced and healthy for you personally and, most importantly, to do this in a way that causes you to become more fully alive instead of drained or burned out. This may sound like an extremely ambitious goal, but I've found that for many men and women it is quite possible to live a life of consistent personal growth and sufficient involvement in "repair the world" projects that are meaningful and fulfilling. The key to doing both of these energizing goals and not becoming overloaded requires that you take to heart a very wise Jewish teaching that is almost two thousand years old but is extremely useful in the 21st century.

The Daily Reminder of How to Stay Balanced and Positive
Around the year 100 CE, in the city of Yavneh (which is 12 miles south of Jaffa and 7 miles east of the Mediterranean Sea in what is now the coastal region of Israel), there were many scholarly

debates and profound teachers, including a well-respected sage named Rabbi Tarfon. He is most remembered for several insightful teachings and sayings, especially his comments about finding what today we would call "the sweet spot" between the two extremes of trying to do more than is humanly possible or reverting to the opposite extreme of giving up altogether on the inner repair and outer repair that your soul is drawn toward during this lifetime.

Rabbi Tarfon's famous quote which you can say to yourself as a daily or weekly focusing method whenever you are starting to feel overloaded, stressed or frustrated during a delay or a setback, is, "You are not obligated to complete the work, but neither are you free to abandon it."

Let's break this down into specific steps in order to understand why it is so centering, positive, and useful, especially for anyone who desires to improve oneself and the world around you without slipping repeatedly into burnout or discouragement:

Step One: Looking at Your Inner Changes as an Ongoing Work-in-Process

Most people are in a hurry to fix whatever is challenging to them and they get very frustrated with themselves if the fix doesn't happen quickly. For example, if you have been trying to improve the way you deal with food, anger, fears, insecurities, or how impatient you are with certain people you live with or work with, you might have noticed that change and improvement tend to be very slow and not always smooth or dependable. One day you think you have mastered your personal issues about food, anger, fears, insecurities, or impatience but then a little while later a new challenging situation shows up and you discover you still have more work to do on this issue.

Does that mean you are a failure at improving this character trait you have been working on for months or decades? No, you are not a failure. You are a human being who like all other human beings has moments of forward progress and moments of slipping back a bit.

If you take a few seconds each day or each week to breathe in gently and consider the sensible approach of Rabbi Tarfon's words ("You are not obligated to complete the work, but neither are you free to abandon it") as applied to your inner work to improve your character traits and habits, then you will probably develop a more loving and enduring approach in the way you treat yourself and your personal challenges.

When you say to yourself Rabbi Tarfon's gentle reminder of "Don't expect 100% completion but do keep going forward as much as possible," then during a moment when you slip or miss the mark, you can say to yourself, "Hey relax. Your job is not to be 100% perfect, 100% complete, or 100% done with all this inner work." In fact, if you were 100% done you'd probably be dead. Your job is to keep going and keep learning more about what it takes for you as a unique human being to make an additional step of progress one day at a time.

Here's a brief example of what Rabbi Tarfon was referring to when he said essentially, "Be loving to yourself and don't hold your breath expecting completion or perfection on goals that take many years and many layers of digging in order to reach completion." The example I want to offer you is one person who discovered how to stop criticizing herself for not being perfect and instead she learned to appreciate the dignity and integrity of facing the fact that all of us have additional things to learn at every stage of life.

The Woman Who Grew Up Being Pressured and Bombarded with Advice

I once had a smart and hard-working client named Diana who grew up with a very controlling set of parents. Diana's mom and dad were not only "helicopter parents" who hovered over her, but also at times they were "vulture parents" who swooped in and critiqued her every decision in a harsh and demeaning way.

After a turbulent time during the first few years after she graduated from college, Diana did some excellent inner work during her 20's to shake off the negative impact of her controlling parents and to become her own trusted decision-maker. But then in her 30's, Diana found herself feeling trapped and demeaned by an extremely controlling but also very romantic partner who was sometimes hyper-critical and frequently quite condescending to her. So Diana did a second round of inner work to understand how to deal with a romantic partner who is a bit too invasive, perfectionistic, and advice-giving.

Then in her 40's, Diana discovered that some of her "I don't want to be controlled" issues were flaring up again regarding a work colleague who was highly demanding and frequently intimidating. So Diana did a third round of inner work on how her early experiences with her parents were impacting her recent experiences with this complicated work colleague.

During one of our counseling sessions, Diana was feeling frustrated that, "I always hoped I had put my issues about my mom and dad behind me. But I feel like a fool that my old issues keep flaring up at various chapters in my life. Is there something wrong with me that I can't seem to be done and finally complete once and for all with these issues?"

At that moment, it occurred to me to talk with Diana about Rabbi Tarfon's famous quote, "You are not obligated to complete the work, but neither are you free to abandon it." We discussed the fact that for most men and women who are doing an excellent job of learning and growing to repair the wounds of childhood, there are definitely going to be a few themes and a few issues that show up again and again at each decade of life. It doesn't mean you are doing something wrong or that you're a defective learner. Instead it usually means you are peeling off deeper and deeper levels of a core theme that requires additional insights and supports at each stage of adult life.

As I explained to Diana, "I think it's important to have a sense of humor and a willingness to embrace the fact that certain issues and themes are going to keep showing up whether you are in your 20's, 30's, 40's, 50's, 60's, 70's or 80's.   It's perfectly ok to peel off a layer from the past and do some great inner work, but then to find a few years later you get challenged in a new way with that same theme or issue, which means you then get a chance to go deeper this next time.   That is the moment to bring in your sense of humor as you can say to yourself (in the playful style of Dana Carvey's character from "Saturday Night Live"), "Well isn't that special, here comes my favorite old issue again and I get another chance to learn from it."   Or you can say to yourself, "Thank goodness I still have some more layers of inner work to do.   Otherwise I'd be six feet under."

Appreciating Your Own Personal Layers of Discovery and Partial Progress

For a moment, let's see how this Rabbi Tarfon perspective of "showing up consistently and not abandoning the inner work" can apply to you and your own life right now. Think about some theme, issue, or challenge in your own daily experiences that you've been trying to change or improve about yourself for many years. It might be how you deal with pushy or difficult people. Or how you handle food, health issues, or fitness routines. Or how you deal with specific fears, doubts, and insecurities. Or how you have wanted to get better at following through on your goals and good ideas, even when there are distractions or interruptions. Or how you have been seeking to become a more patient and compassionate person with loved ones or with people you meet out in the world.

Now visualize for a moment one of the layers you have peeled away already and sorted out the first time you began working on this particular issue.   What were the discoveries and break-throughs you uncovered the first time you went "digging" in these muddy areas of your life?

Then visualize the additional layers you peeled away and sorted out the most recent time you worked on this issue, theme, or challenge.   What did you figure out and begin to change or improve the last time you poked at this issue from a slightly more advanced perspective?   What were the signs of progress that came from this most recent inner work?

Now visualize the next layers you hope to peel away and sort out in the coming days, weeks or months as you take another honest look at this theme or issue. If you get additional support, tools and focus on this recurring theme, then imagine what kind of progress you will make in this next round.

This step-by-step, one chapter-at-a-time appreciation for the ongoing process of doing inner work is what Rabbi Tarfon had the wisdom to offer us in his statement, "It is not your obligation to complete the work, but neither are you free to abandon it."   The next time you are feeling frustrated or you are tempted to give up on a self-improvement quest, say these words to yourself and utilize them to bounce back into a state of openness to additional growth and progress.

I will admit that I can't stop you from beating yourself up if you tend to have a brain that makes self-critical comments like, "What's taking so long for me to change" or "Why do I keep having to go over the same themes again and again."   It's a free country and you have the right to beat yourself up if you desire.

But from a Jewish perspective, you are lovingly invited and en-couraged every day, every week, and every year to treat yourself with kindness and caring as you seek to re-align your individual actions with the awesome flow and wisdom of the Creative Source (or the still small voice within). In Judaism there is never a moment when it's too late to turn in a more holy direction and reconnect with the higher purpose and unique beauty of your pure soul. Please don't use up your precious energy criticizing yourself for not being perfect or 100% done growing. Rather, with a Yiddish accent you can say to yourself, "You should live a long life," because it does take a long life to keep making progress on the complicated layers of inner work that each of us has in front of us no matter what age we are at the moment.

Step Two: Looking at Your "Repair the World" Involvements from a Healthier Perspective
In the 1560's there was a brilliant teacher named Rabbi Isaac Luria in Safed (pronounced Tzi-faht in Hebrew, it is a beautiful town in the northern part of Israel above the Sea of Galilee). Luria talked in depth about "tikkun olam," repairing the shattered or broken aspects of the world, and for more than 450 years since then Jews have been expanding on his teachings and being quite active in many varieties of improving what's unjust, what's insensitive, and what's in need of repair in this world we share.

But if you have ever gotten immersed in a passionate effort to repair something that's broken in the environmental realm, or in a political situation, or in the place where you work, live, or go to school, you probably know that three things tend to happen:

- it usually takes a lot more time, energy, and commitment than you knew at first.
- it often requires more teamwork, consensus-building, and consciousness-raising than you ever imagined.
- it sometimes means that you start feeling so self-righteous and passionate about the causes you are fighting for that you might fall into the trap of alienating or turning off people who would otherwise be your allies if you weren't being so rigidly righteous and preachy.

Does that ring true about yourself or anyone you know? Have you ever witnessed a well-intentioned "do-gooder" who got swept up in a cause that turned out to be more than he or she had bargained for, or that caused this individual to become self-righteous, insufferable, or burned out to the point of losing one's health or one's connection to various friends and family?

As a therapist who frequently counsels non-profit organizations and numerous men and women who are "do-gooders," (and as a bit of an activist myself), I have found that there can sometimes be an unhealthy "shoot yourself in the foot" way to pursue tikkun olam. On the other hand, if you bring to mind the teachings of Rabbi Tarfon that "it is not your obligation to complete the work but neither are you free to abandon it," then you can begin to develop a much healthier and more successful way of repairing some corner of the world.

Here are a few brief illustrations of what I mean by using Rabbi Tarfon's sensible mantra which I will paraphrase as, "Don't get all twisted up and exhausted by the task of improving the world, but rather find a way to do it with lovingkindness, creative teamwork, and the joy of being part of the gradual but never-ending repair of this amazing world."

ILLUSTRATION A: The Woman Who Kept Getting Twisted in Knots from Trying to Do Too Much

Dalia is a passionate environmentalist who has known since she was a teenager that she wanted to heal some of the broken aspects of the world's ecology. But she's also someone who has gotten physically ill and emotional drained several times in recent years because she tends to get roped into exhausting non-stop committee meetings, sit-ins, demonstrations, and fundraising efforts.

During one of our counseling sessions, when I discussed with Dalia what Rabbi Tarfon suggested, which is essentially, "Don't try to do it all, but don't settle for doing less than you can," Dalia got inspired to choose more carefully which meetings to shorten or do calmly from home with Skype or Face Time, which physically-draining events to skip in order to stay healthy, and what kinds of projects and fundraising efforts could be done with less physical strain and more supportive teamwork.

As Dalia explained to me on her final day of counseling, "I'm still a passionate environmentalist. But I'm also a lot smarter now about how to choose the activities that keep me from getting drained or sick, and how to say 'No' to the time-wasting activities that used to tax my body too much or that were filled with too much unnecessary drama."

If you have ever jeopardized your physical or emotional health by your willingness to go along with all sorts of martyr-like "save the world" scenarios, now might be a good time to consider, "What can I do to be more balanced between the part of me that wants to be of service to an important cause and the part of me that is discovering I have physical and emotional sensitivities that cannot be ignored or I will not be able to hang in there for the long haul?" Repairing the world takes endurance and the best way to prepare yourself for that endurance is to make sure you don't burn out or act like a martyr. The world needs you to be healthy, creative, and persistent...not to be physically or emotionally wiped out by throwing yourself into avoidable toxic situations.

ILLUSTRATION B: The Leader Who Began to Find Time to Be with the People Who Were Missing Him

Jake is a busy accountant and business manager who has a wife and three children. So he doesn't have a huge amount of time for volunteer activities. But because he has a lot of ideas and energy, Jake often gets selected to be the leader of various groups—his condo association, the social action committee of his professional networking group, the annual community service project of the local chapter of his college alumni association, and the tikkun olam (repairing the world) committee at his temple.

Recently, Jake heard from his wife and his kids during a counseling session that they miss him terribly and they wish he would spend more time with them. At first Jake felt frustrated, as he commented, "Can't anyone see that I'm a person who wants to give back to the world." To which his wife Sally replied, "How about giving back to the people who love you and miss you."

During that same counseling session, I asked Jake and his wife Sally to view themselves as cooperative teammates on a game show called, "Finding the Balance Between Enjoyable Family Time and Worthwhile Outside Involvements." Both Jake and Sally smiled as Jake admitted, "We've never viewed this as a cooperative topic. It's usually a power struggle about whether 'family time' or 'helping the world' projects are going to win the scheduling wars."

But as soon as they began brainstorming together as creative teammates on an imaginary game show, what Jake and many others have discovered is that setting aside time for family closeness doesn't destroy the possibility of repairing the wider world or being involved in important causes. But it did help Jake learn to say "No" to requests that were pulling him away from the people he loved and to delegate more to other people who could do what he does (though not as well, of course).

Jake's still a dependable leader at two of the five groups he used to lead, but by pulling back a bit at the other groups, he's freed up several hours a week for family time that has made his wife and kids extremely grateful to be with him. As Jake's wife Sally described during one of their final counseling sessions, "Jake is still passionate about these outside involvements that do a lot for the world. But he's also becoming more passionate and more available for our family. So I'm able to appreciate that he's a good person with a lot to give and at the same time he's more balanced and less stressed now that he's learned to let go of some of those fancy titles and let others step up to do some of the time-consuming leadership responsibilities."

In your own life, is there a loved one, family member, or friend who is currently missing you and wishing you could come up for air sometimes rather than being immersed constantly in your "repair the world" projects?   Is there a balanced way to let go of a portion of the things that are on your "I'm the Only One Who Can Do It" list so that you can create some beautiful moments with this loved one, this family member, or this friend who needs your caring and companionship?

ILLUSTRATION C: The Wise Person Who Realized It's About Empowering Future Generations

Maura, a film producer and the dedicated mom of two young children, decided several years ago (after seeing a documentary film that moved her deeply) that she wanted to do something about the rights of young women in poor countries to be able to get a good education.

According to Maura, "I was in tears when I saw the vast number of girls and young women who simply aren't allowed to get an education or who have to miss a lot of school because they have to do exhausting jobs (often with only minimal pay or no pay at all) to support their families."

As a result, Maura got involved in two non-profit groups that attempt to make an impact on societies where girls and young women are held back by laws or traditions that block millions of individuals who happen to be female from becoming educated, self-supporting, or free to make choices in life.

At first Maura was excited to be involved in something so meaningful and inspiring. But after several years of doing a tremendous amount of fundraising, political lobbying, and arranging big events for this important cause, Maura found, "I was starting to get discouraged and feeling somewhat hopeless.   The problem keeps getting bigger and in many parts of the world the societal push-back seems to be getting more vicious."

During one of her counseling sessions, I explored with Maura what kind of revised strategy and increased endurance she might be able to develop if she used Rabbi Tarfon's quote as a daily mantra. Maura admitted, "I've never really stepped back and asked how to do this important work in a way that will keep me healthy, balanced, and positive for the long haul."

But when she began to inspire herself each week with the phrase, "You are not obligated to complete the work, but neither are you free to abandon it," Maura started to get some new ideas on how to be more effective and fulfilled by her efforts on behalf of young women and girls in oppressive societies.

One morning, Maura was sitting at breakfast and thinking about the words of Rabbi Tarfon and she realized, "I have been wearing myself out trying to create immediate changes in political, religious, and social systems that are thousands of years old. What if I stopped being in such a hurry and I started looking at how to build a slower but more viable change strategy in these reluctant societies?"

With the help of one of her close friends, Maura began to design an "Unstoppable Mentoring Program" in which activists in their 30's, 40's and 50's could train, inspire, and empower activists in their teens and 20's about how to carry on the passion and good work of getting more people from various parts of these societies involved in standing up for the rights of girls and young women. She began to reach out and include a variety of new allies from within these countries who shared her views but were also more savvy about how actual change and progress take place in highly-traditional cultures.

According to Maura, "I'm no longer focusing on the short-term ups and downs of trying to fix this quickly or else fall into despair. Instead I'm constantly building several generations of people from all levels of these societies who are committed to changing this awful situation. I feel more effective and alive almost every day because I'm seeing just how many people of various ages and backgrounds are getting involved in small or large ways."

With this mantra of "Don't over-focus on the immediate results, but do stay involved for the long-term transformations," Maura and many other men and women have found they are healthier and more energized to keep repairing some crucial aspect of life on Earth. I hope that this non-rushed but highly-strategic perspective will help you in your own "repair the world" projects as well.

ILLUSTRATION D: The Man Who Stopped Being a Turnoff and Started Being More Effective

Finally, there is one more key issue that can help balance the desire to repair the world and the need to work on one's own character traits and habits. One of my colleagues, a brilliant teacher and blog writer named Randy, is passionate about the rights of those who are differently abled. For years Randy was active in numerous groups and causes, but each time he found himself battling with the leadership of those groups over what was "too radical" and what was "too cautious." In addition, Randy felt alienated from his family, from many of his friends, and from most of his work colleagues because, in his words, "Whenever I open my mouth about what I'm passionate about, I'm told that my intensity tends to suck the air out of the room. Even if people agree with what I'm saying, they tell me sooner or later that they are put off by my abrasive tone and my huge judgmentalness."

One day Randy and I went to lunch and I asked him a question that I have asked many activists from a variety of different causes and programs. I said, "I truly care about you and I truly want your efforts to be successful. But since I'm not as fully knowledgeable as you are about what it's like to live each day as a person who is differently abled, I need your help sometimes. Would you be willing to tell me in a caring voice whenever I say something uninformed or insensitive that gets on your nerves?   Would you be willing to treat me as an ally and not as an adversary or an idiot, even when I clumsily say or do something you don't like?"

My friend Randy looked surprised as he admitted, "You want me to ask nicely without being judgmental--I've never even considered that as a possibility. I am so passionate about what I'm fighting for...it never occurred to me that there's a gentle and calm way to bring people in rather than to push them aside with my passionate lecturing.   I can't promise I'll do a perfect job of never using a harsh tone with you.   But I'll do what I can."

That was the beginning of a breakthrough in our friendship and in this amazing activist's work.   He no longer seemed so furious and impatient whenever things weren't 100% the way he wanted them to be.   When we were discussing various strategies on how to improve things for individuals who are physically challenged or cognitively diverse in the Jewish community and in the wider community, he now was able to draw from a much wider range of ideas on how to inspire people, how to bring out the best in people, and how to help people open up their hearts and minds in ways they never have before.

In your own "repair the world" moments, have you also lashed out occasionally at someone who was a potential ally but this person was also somewhat clumsy or less-than-perfect in the way he or she was dealing with your particular issue?   Is there some subtle way that your tone of voice, your flashes of judgmental dismissiveness, or your self-righteousness have pushed away certain men and women who actually wanted to give support to your cause?

Now might be a good moment to ask yourself, "What if I reminded myself to 'stop focusing on 100% perfect completion of the work' and yet I can still stay involved in a more compassionate and less judgmental way?   What if I stopped expecting 100% compliance from people and started to appreciate that lots of individuals might have a variety of ways of adding to the support my cause will be needing?   What if I lightened up on the pressure to make each person a clone of who I am and started letting them be who they are in pursuit of the same worthwhile goals?"

It just might happen that the more you do your inner work to repair the parts of you that are impatient, judgmental, or rigid, then the more it will improve your effectiveness in repairing what's broken in the world.   Instead of turning off the people who would like to help you reach your vision for repairing some aspect of life on Earth, you will be adding numerous allies and approaches to the momentum toward change and progress.

CHAPTER 7

ENJOYING MINI-SABBATICALS EACH DAY AND EACH WEEK

During the fall and winter of 2014-2015, there was a song on the radio in which the female singer Colbie Caillat talked about how hard we all "try, try, try" in order to be enough, do enough, look good enough, and prove we are worthy enough.

Do you ever feel that way? Do you ever sense that your body or your mind are on "High Effort Mode" or "High Vigilance Mode" too much of the time without sufficient relief moments for letting go, unwinding, or feeling free of constant pressures and uncertainties.

In Judaism there is a brilliant and effective remedy for this. But in order to understand how it works, you might need to look at this possible remedy from a fresh perspective.

A New Look at a Timeless Idea
When you think of the word "Sabbath" or "Shabbat," what comes to mind for you? In your honest opinion, is it:
   (please feel free to check one or more of these possibilities)

- a list of overly-strict rules about what you should do or cannot do on the seventh day.

- a gateway to a feeling of delicious release from the pressures of your busy life.
- a rehearsal for what life would be like if everyone had enough food, love, and joy so that no one felt "less than enough."
- a chance to stop trying to prove yourself in the world, but to appreciate the gifts and wisdom that no stressor can take away from you.
- a sense of connecting with something timeless and holy in which Jews all over the world are sharing a profound experience that has sustained us continually for centuries.
- a rare opportunity to stop rushing and instead to move gently at a different, slower pace.
- a nice idea in theory that unfortunately you are too busy to practice most of the time.

I hope you were honest with yourself. I hope that whatever your opinion is right now about the words "Sabbath" or "Shabbat," you are willing to look at it carefully.

In this seventh and final chapter of "More Fully Alive," I will be offering you a way to understand and experience the deeper realities of "Sabbath" or "Shabbat" from a perspective you might not have considered before. It's a perspective that's not so much about "the rules," but much more about nourishing your soul and re-connecting with your true essence. Are you interested in something fairly easy and accessible that can strongly reconnect you with your soul's essence and re-energize the life force within you? If so, please continue reading.

A Quick Experiment
To understand with new awareness what the words "Sabbath" or "Shabbat" mean on a deeper level, let's do an unusual experiment. For a few seconds, take in a strong and full inhale but don't exhale (for as long as you can). Hold the breath a little longer. A little longer. Only breathe when you must...

What does that feel like? To what extent do you experience the tightness, the rigidity, the frustration, or the sense of discomfort from inhaling intensely without exhaling?

What if you were to live your life by being all-inhale and no-exhale, or all-effort and no-release?

In Judaism there is a back-and-forth rhythm of inhaling lovingly and exhaling lovingly that is essential to becoming more fully alive. There is a beautiful respect in many of the scholarly writings about the Sabbath for appreciating the back-and-forth rhythm of intense activity (the deep inhale) followed by an equally important release and renewal (the liberating exhale).

This balancing of the effortful parts of life followed by an effortless sense of letting go into a state of gratitude and awe were first described way back in the original writings in Genesis and Exodus. That's where we first read about the Ultimate Creative Source (a mystery that we can only speculate about and never quite describe sufficiently), which did something surprising and notable while slowly turning the unformed chaos of the world into planets, oceans, land forms, vegetation, birds, insects, animals, food sources, and humans.

Here's what it says in Genesis and Exodus about the back-and-forth rhythm of intense activity followed by an equally important exhale:

According to the text, during each segment of time (which usually gets translated as the "seven days of creation" but most rabbis and scholars describe it as "seven lengthy periods of time"), there was an intense burst of creativity and effort, followed by a pause and a moment of reflection in which the One doing the creating "saw that it was good." Think about it and consider whether your own creative process consists of a pause to breathe and notice what is going right (instead of just what is still unfinished or uncertain). What would your life be like if every day or every week there was a pause, a deep breath in and out, and a chance to notice, "There's a lot of good here in the midst of the chaos."

Then during the next segment of time, there was another intense burst of creativity and effort, followed by a pause and a moment of reflection in which the One doing the creating "saw that it was good." You can see a pattern emerging—intense activity and creativity followed by a pause to notice what's good, and then to refresh before the next burst of activity.

Then according to the ancient text, there was a surprising and startling next phase in which there was a substantial pause to let go and to refresh in a more significant way.

If you look at the original Hebrew words (for instance in Exodus 31:17) it describes this important exhale for letting go, refreshing, and reconnecting with one's essence as, "Shavvat Va-yinafash," which has been translated a number of ways by scholars and rabbis over the years, including Rashi, Nachmanides, Samson Raphael Hirsch, Abraham Joshua Heschel, and others. I am going to list several of these various translations for you and I'll let you select which one you would like to use as your personal mantra or refreshing reminder cue whenever you want to engage in the exquisite experience of "Shavvat va-yinafash."

What exactly does "Shavvat va-yinafash" mean in English? Take a moment to think about each of these possible translations in terms of your own life as a busy person who has bursts of creativity and effort, followed by (hopefully) a moment to notice what is good and beautiful, and then another burst of creativity and effort followed by another moment of (hopefully) noticing what is good and beautiful. After several rounds of intense effort and activity, you can then exhale with the words "Shavvat va-yinafash," which can mean (according to various commentators and teachers from the past two thousand years who have written on this key phrase):

"And he (or she) rested from all labors" (Here the word "shav-vat" or "Shabbat" is translated as "resting from labors")

Or: "And she rested and re-connected with her soul" (here the emphasis is making sure you connect with your nefesh/soul, which is the root word found in va-yinafash)"

Or: "And this moment of letting go is restoring his soul" (shav-vat or Shabbat also means "let go and restore," while va-yinafash/ nefesh refers to the "soul")

Or: "This release from effort and worldly activity restores my spiritual essence"

Or: "This time set apart from pressure and effort re-connects me to my true spirit"

Or: "As I let go of the striving and stress, I return to the soul level of existence."

As you look at these different phrases one more time in order to select one of the phrases to try out in your own life, which of the above translations do you think might be able to give you a definite feeling of release and renewal? What would it mean to you personally if you said this particular phrase to yourself after an intense day or an intense week? As you reflect on the words "Shavvat va-yinafash," you are letting go of the striving and stress for a specific amount of time so that you can re-connect with your true self, your spiritual self, your soul's timeless essence. As you close your eyes and breathe calmly in and out while saying the words "Shavvat va-yinafash" after a day or a week of intense inhales and effort, you are letting go and restoring your soul and your life force with a gentle and loving exhale.

I have seen this phrase be extremely helpful for many of my counseling clients and in my own life as well. I've found repeat-edly that when I say to myself, "Shavvat va-yinafash," and I take a few deep breaths in and out, I often translate it as "Letting go of effort and stress. Letting the soul be renewed again." If I breathe calmly in and out as I say it in Hebrew and English silently, it seems to take me to a place deep inside where there is a sense of peacefulness and an inspiring connection to something that I cannot put in words.

The Weekly Opportunity to Transform Your Energy

Starting at sundown on every Friday night for many centuries, Jews from all over the world have engaged in a fascinating step-by-step process of "Shavvat va-yinafash, resting and renewing one's soul"—a carefully designed process of shifting your energies from the stressfulness of the weekdays and opening up to the beauty and spirituality of Shabbat, the seventh day.

But before we begin to explore the specifics of how this can happen in a positive way for you and your family, I have to admit something controversial. Like many people today, I grew up hearing a lot of men and women complaining that the rules of Shabbat were too rigid and restrictive. At the somewhat-Conservative/somewhat-Orthodox shul in Detroit which I attended often with my beloved grandfather when I was a pre-teen and teenager, I frequently heard congregants kvetching that keeping the Sabbath was "a burden." But like soldiers who complain about the excessive rules and regulations of their cherished platoon, the complaining seemed to have a sense of pride and loyalty to it, as if the congregants were saying, "Yes it's a burden of rules and restrictions, but we wouldn't have it any other way."

At the Reform temple in Detroit that I also attended frequently with my immediate family and on my own for many years, there was also a lot of kvetching but these complaints were somewhat different. Many of the congregants at this very progressive and innovative temple didn't follow most of the Sabbath rules and many viewed Shabbat as an outdated relic that was no longer relevant to their lives. The feeling in those years among many seemed to be that rebelling against the many rules of Shabbat was a way of saying, "I am an ultra-modern Jew." I was fascinated by the contrasts in these two sizeable congregations—one that leaned toward "compliance" and one that leaned toward "rebelliousness."

It took many years before I found out from various other rabbis, teachers, friends, colleagues, study groups, readings, and personal experiences that the Jewish Sabbath is not really about leaning toward "compliance" or leaning toward "rebelliousness." Rather, it's something on another dimension--quite mystical, holy, healthful, delicious and profound. It eventually became one of the most enjoyable and meaningful parts of my life and a source of joy and closeness for my immediate family and friends during my adult years.

The Personal Invitation Gift Certificate
Now imagine in your own life that the sun is starting to go down and it's Friday night after an especially stressful week. Instead of thinking about Shabbat as a difficult maze of rules, restrictions, and burdens…what if you looked at it with new eyes and a sense of new curiosity (whether you consider yourself Orthodox, Conservative, Reform, Reconstructionist, Renewal, Secular, or none of the above).

For example, what if you walked into your home and you saw a beautifully wrapped gift certificate on your kitchen table that invites you to enjoy a special and unique day that is to be devoted entirely to the care of your exquisite soul. On that special day you do not have to work or do any heavy lifting. You can take a walk and have a relaxing conversation with friends or loved ones about the things that really matter. You can meditate, pray, and read the books that speak to your soul. You can nap, cuddle with a loved one, or dance and sing to let your spirit soar.

For one day, you can stop trying to prove yourself out in the world. You can look at your life as a blessing and feel at peace with where you are right now. Instead of feeling fragmented and pressured, you can spend the day in a generous, positive, and grateful mood.

Learning how to make the Sabbath into a day for breaking free of the pressures of your life (and finding a peaceful connection to your inner spirit) might not happen completely the first few times you attempt it. You might find it interesting that this "Invitation Gift Certificate" has no expiration date on it and so it can be used as many times as you would like starting as soon as you are ready to begin exploring what it offers you.

The other thing that is quite interesting about this gift certificate is that you can utilize a small part of it, a large part of it, or almost all of it. You might go several weeks or months testing out just one small portion of the list of possible things that make Shabbat come alive for people near and far. It's not a race or a contest, but rather a chance to practice the art of letting go and unhooking from the pressures of the week so that you can allow your soul to be cared for more lovingly. Some people take a few years and others an entire lifetime before they develop the full ability to let go and just be. Please don't be stressed about whether you're progressing quickly enough toward a "100% perfect Sabbath" and please don't be in a competition with anyone who's having an easier time of it. After all, it's Shabbat...a day to breathe in and out from a place of feeling grateful that "There's some good here despite the chaos. There's a holiness here in letting go of the pressure to be more, do more, or have more."

Choosing One or Two Small Steps Toward a Balanced Life
If you are somewhat curious about how to nourish your soul once a week and connect to a beautiful sense of "What would it be like to live in a timeless and grateful state of mind, where there is abundant food, love, music, transcendence, deep conversations, and calmness," then you can begin by taking one or two steps at a time to shift your over-stressed life into a more healthful direction.

As you breathe in and out while saying to yourself, "Shavvat va-yinafash, let go and let the soul be refreshed," the first one or two steps of a weekly Shabbat might be:

- **Bring in Some Light.** Even if you and your family members didn't light Shabbat candles when you were growing up, you can start whenever you want. Just close your eyes, let your swaying hands feel the energy moving to surround you and your dinner mates lovingly, and then breathe in and out as you say a blessing for the lights of the candles and the spiritual light that is within us and around us. If you feel awkward or uncertain about how to do this, have a friend, relative, or rabbi show you how. Each time you do this on a Friday night, you might notice that the energy in the room changes in subtle ways once the candles begin to glow. Your exhausted mood might begin to lift somewhat. You might also find that the invisible connections between those present in the room (and those who are not in the room but who are in your heart and memory) are profound and inspiring.
- **Notice How You Walk and Talk.** Since Shabbat is about experiencing the timelessness and peacefulness that we sometimes fail to see during the busy weekdays, you might notice there is a more loving and gentle way of moving, conversing, enjoying each bite of some delicious food, and interacting more comfortably on Shabbat. Shabbat asks the question, "What would it feel like if there were peace in the world, peace within our families, and peace inside of us?" Many scholars describe Shabbat as a rehearsal for "What would the world be like if we all treated each other more lovingly and more patiently? What would the world be like if we all had enough and we weren't trying so hard to have more or be more?" As you take a relaxing walk on Shabbat

or as you engage in a non-rushed conversation or meal with someone you care about, notice how it feels different from the often-hurried interactions of the weekdays.

- **Choose a Few Things to Say "Yes" and Enjoy.** Many people were raised with a lot of "No's" and restrictions about what was forbidden on Shabbat. But if you turn it around and ask yourself, "What do I want to say 'Yes' about on this day of awe, wonder, and gratitude," see what pops up as possibilities. Is there a spiritual book or article that you've wanted to read but were too busy on workdays—so now on Shabbat you have the time to go deeper into the curiosities of your soul? Is there some sacred dance, inspiring music, or connection to nature that you don't have time to enjoy during the week, but on Shabbat there is a timelessness that allows your spiritual energy to increase? Is there a special someone with whom you would like to hold hands, make eye contact, cuddle, or make love? On Shabbat it is considered a double blessing to be in a timeless soul connection with a loved one.

Is there a particular food or dessert that you would like to enjoy as a special treat on this special day? Is there a story about a cherished parent, grandparent, teacher, or friend that you want to share with the next generation? Is there something for which you are grateful, awe-struck, curious, or personally moved that you would like to discuss with the people you live with or the ones that you invite to a Shabbat meal? Is there someone you would like to thank, appreciate, encourage, or laugh with on this day that is set apart from the other days?

Once again, I'm not saying you have to do it 100% correctly or change your lifestyle immediately and forever. You probably will have some questions, concerns, joys, hesitations, and personalized choices about how to make Shabbat come alive for you in a way that nourishes your soul and the souls of the people you care about. All I'm asking is that you consider the possibility that a profound exhale and a sense of peacefulness will add to your sense of being fully alive.   Please don't worry about trying to do Shabbat exactly like someone else does Shabbat--you can decide who to consult with and how to select the particular details and flavors of how you would like to make this a joyous and nourishing part of your life. For example, here are two quick illustrations of how Shabbat can be done in a unique and different way depending on who you are and what nourishes your particular soul.

The Woman Who Wasn't Sure About Being Called a Priestess
One of my colleagues is a woman named Zoey who grew up in a secular Jewish household where religious rituals and practices were considered "old fashioned" and "no longer useful."   So Zoey steered away from Jewish groups and activities. Yet she felt a long-ing in her soul for something spiritual and, as a result, she got involved after college in an alternative spiritual group from a dif-ferent tradition that was focused on empowering women to be spiritual leaders.

Zoey was quite active for a while with this group.   But she eventually pulled away when her life got extra busy with work and family demands.

Then a few years ago I mentioned to Zoey about a workshop I was going to be attending on "The Priestess Traditions in Judaism," in which the workshop leader was going to be talking about and demonstrating how the Shabbat rituals (such as lighting the can-dles, setting a beautiful altar of soft fabrics and sacred objects, blessing the gathered guests and family members, offering some wisdom about life and what is most meaningful to her) was actu-ally a way of keeping Judaism alive 2,000 years ago after the de-struction of the ancient temples in Jerusalem and bringing these rituals into the home, often with female leadership of the Shabbat ritual practices. In the opinion of some scholars, these Shabbat practices in the home were part of the Jewish priestess tradition which has been a part of Judaism for thousands of years.

Zoey looked at me with skepticism when I first told her about this workshop. "Oh yeah, right, a Jewish priestess," she remarked. "I'll believe it when I see it."

But at this and other workshops, Zoey and many others have discovered that yes, in fact, the Shabbat rituals have always been an opportunity for women to be the channels of holy energies and the ones who bring a sense of sacredness and shared wisdom to the friends and family members gathered together. Yes there has been a lot of sexism in Judaism and other religions, but there is also a long history of female empowerment and feminist wisdom in the Jewish world.

That conversation was the spark which caused Zoey to begin reconnecting with her Judaism from a Jewish feminist perspective. She eventually began putting together and enjoying a meaningful Shabbat nearly every Friday night and on many Saturdays. She began meeting numerous women and men who were also exploring non-traditional ways to make Shabbat come alive for progressive individuals in the 21st century.

Zoey told me a few months ago, "I'm still not sure I'm willing to call myself a priestess. It's a bit much for a social worker like myself to use a fancy title like that. But I do feel an amazing sense of gratitude and timeless connection each time I bring in the light, make my guests feel welcome, and I lead the conversations that go deep almost every time for each of the people gathered at my Friday night table. I had no idea there was so much good stuff to be found in doing Shabbat on a consistent basis. Yet I'm so glad to have it in my life now because it enriches not only my weekends but also gives me a spiritual boost that carries over into the weekdays."

The Introvert Who Found a Sense of Connection

Kurt is a therapy client who first came in for a session when his wife was suffering from cancer and he stayed in therapy to work on his sense of grief and frustration at losing the remarkable individual he called "the best friend I've ever had."

Since Kurt is a somewhat shy and private person, he wasn't sure what he wanted to do about the extreme aloneness he was experiencing after the death of his wife. According to Kurt, "I am not a joiner. I don't feel comfortable in large groups where people are engaged in small talk or tooting their horns. I'd rather be at home with a book or a TV remote clicker."

But after two years of being a widower and turning down all sorts of overtures from neighborhood women who brought him casseroles and invitations to go to movies, Kurt asked me one week, "Isn't there some way to be connected to other people, but to still have a sense of independence and privacy?"

That was the beginning of some brainstorming conversations in which we explored what would be the right amount of connection that Kurt might enjoy (and what would be too much for his preferred way of interacting). One of the ideas that Kurt was willing to test out was for him to go to a nearby congregation that had a small discussion group about ethics and integrity issues each Saturday morning during the hour prior to Shabbat services.

What Kurt found there is, "A small and mostly decent group of people who are willing to talk about things that matter and they don't try to shove anything down your throat. Then after the discussion group, I enjoy being part of their lively singing at their Shabbat services. It's just a couple hours a week, but it gets me into a completely different mindset than how I am on most other days. I find I like the sense of spirituality and the chance to talk about deeper issues. No one forces me to talk when I don't want to talk. And when I do open up and say something, there seems to be a mutual respect that we're all human and we're all looking for ways to deepen our values and our connection to something bigger than just our egos and routines."

If you are like Kurt and you've never considered yourself a "joiner" or someone who likes to follow the crowd, I hope you will still look around to find the Shabbat study group or the Shabbat celebration style that feels right to you. You'll know it is a good decision if you find it nourishes your soul more often than not. We are fortunate to be living in a time when there are many choices and many diverse styles for how people want to get together and connect with what's meaningful at Shabbat gatherings.

So what happened to Kurt once he joined a congregation? If this were an American movie, I would tell you now that Kurt met his bashert (his soul mate) at one of these Shabbat study groups and they lived happily ever after. But in fact this true story is more like a foreign film and Kurt continues to be somewhat of a shy and private person, who nevertheless feels a bit more connected and much more alive because each week he has a place to go where there is a sense of holiness and mutual respect.

As he told me a few weeks ago, "I'm still alone a lot and I'm still not 100% recovered from the loss of my wife. But each Saturday morning I feel a sense of meaning and inspiration when I get involved in the discussions and the singing that take me out of my narrow self. I can honestly say my soul is more energized when the cantor and the congregation are singing and we are together as one people."

The Possibility of a Mini-Sabbatical During a Stressful Weekday
In addition to the benefits of letting go of stress and letting your soul be nourished each Friday night and Saturday, there are also moments during the six other days when you can take a deep inhale and exhale as you say to yourself, "Shavvat va-yinafash, and I am releasing right now from the pressure so that I can feel my soul being nourished."

Here are a few quick examples of how to take a mini-Sabbatical whenever you find yourself being pulled too tightly by all the demands on your time and energy.   See which of the following you do already and which might be helpful if you tried them out every so often:

- Weekday Mini-Sabbatical Possibility #1:   The Ten Minute Mini-Vacation

Lots of people work themselves to exhaustion prior to their one or two week annual vacation and then they get a cold or flu while on vacation.   What if we experimented with a different way of "letting go and taking a vacation?"   What if there were mini-vacations of ten minutes or so every few hours during a busy weekday?

Here's how it works for many people who have tested out this radically different way to increase your health and vitality at key moments during the week.   The ten-minute mini-vacation starts whenever you feel stressed or overloaded and you take a moment to breathe in and out as you say to yourself, "Shavvat va-yinafash, I am going to take a brief moment to rest, to let go, and to nourish my soul."

You can do this by locking the door of your office for just ten minutes, or locking the door of the bathroom stall, or locking the door of your bedroom, or sitting comfortably on a sofa, or a chair, or under a shady tree.   Then set your cell phone alarm or a nearby alarm clock for just 10 minutes.   During those 10 minutes, simply breathe calmly and slowly in and out.   Let your mind wander and don't judge the thoughts that are racing through your brain.   Just let them flow for 10 minutes.   Or let yourself drift into a short refreshing nap of 10 minutes (from which you will probably wake up after the alarm in a very refreshed mood rather than the groggy fogginess that happens for most people when you nap for longer than 30 minutes).

The Over-Cooked Mom
Will ten minutes of pressure-free breathing and rest allow you to unhook from an overfilled day and recharge your batteries

somewhat? We'll only find out if you test it a few times on busy days in your own life. But to give you an approximate idea of what to expect, here's what happened when a mom named Lynnette experimented with the "Ten Minute Mini-Vacation:"

Lynette came to one of my talks at her son's middle school where I had been asked to discuss "Spiritual Methods for Staying Healthy as an Overloaded Parent." Lynette not only has two young children but she also has a growing one-person business of doing public relations consulting and fundraising events for non-profit groups.

According to Lynette, "I used to get so overcooked each day from my kids and from my clients that by late-morning or mid-afternoon I was exhausted because my mind was racing with thoughts of 'how am I ever going to catch up to all the things that I was supposed to do today, but I've had to put most of them on hold because of constant interruptions and delays?'"

When Lynette first heard me talk about the benefits of a mini-sabbatical of ten minutes on a busy day, she laughed and said to her nearby friend, "This guy has got to be kidding. He doesn't know I don't even have time to go to the bathroom."

So when I spoke to her one-on-one during one of the snack breaks and she told me she didn't have enough time for even her essential private needs, I asked her, "Does your bathroom door have a lock on it and would your pre-teen kids be ok if you were in that locked bathroom for ten minutes either before you picked them up from school or while they were doing their homework?"

Lynette looked at me like I was crazy, but I assured her, "I'm the active parent of a child with special needs who has never been able to self-soothe and who needs a lot of focused attention. I appreciate that it's not easy to lock a door when your vulnerable child wants your complete undivided attention all the time. But it's an eye-opener when you discover that just five or ten minutes of quiet and non-pressured time can make you feel alive and resilient again."

Although she was still somewhat skeptical, Lynette experimented for the next few weeks with this idea of a ten minute, eyes closed, relaxing mini-vacation in the middle of a stressful day. She later told me, "It was strange at first. When I said, 'Shavvat va-yinafash, I am letting go and nourishing my soul,' my first thought was, 'No way. Ten minutes with my eyes closed and my breath flowing in and out calmly is not going to make any difference in the stress and fragmentation I am experiencing right now.' And for most of the ten minutes I did have a noisy brain with all sorts of racing thoughts."

Then when her cell phone alarm signaled ten minutes were up, Lynette opened her eyes and noticed, "Despite the fact that my brain was noisy during most of the ten minutes while I was breathing calmly in and out, I opened my eyes again and I was able to focus much better and my nerve endings were a lot less edgy. I wasn't 100% more refreshed but I was re-energized enough that I felt like a human being again instead of a frayed piece of rope. It surprised me that in just ten minutes of breathing and letting my thoughts race freely without judgment I had shifted my energy so noticeably. I went back to being a super-mom and a super-consultant once again with a much stronger sense of presence and strength."

If you are like Lynette was and you aren't sure whether anything as brief as a ten minute mini-sabbatical can make a difference, just try it out a few times and see what happens. See whether your soul enjoys ten minutes of no pressure, no expectations, no judging, and no stress. Then after ten minutes, notice whether you have a little more patience, clarity, and vitality that will come in handy for dealing with your family, your work, and your other responsibilities. At the end of the ten minutes, remind yourself of the ancient words of release, "Shavvat va-yinafash, and she (or he) rested and was renewed."

- Weekday Mini-Sabbatical Possibility #2: The One Hour "Phantom Client"

For many people, it is difficult to follow through and take good care of your own needs (even for a few minutes of mini-sabbatical) when there are so many time pressures, agitated people, and unfinished projects on your mind each day. You might have promised yourself, "I'll set aside a few minutes of quiet, or stretch, or take a refreshing walk around the neighborhood," but then a minute later you feel the urge to "handle just one more thing" or "check the emails or Facebook messages for just a few seconds" and suddenly the mini-sabbatical is vetoed.

Now here's a trick (that has worked for many people from all walks of life) that can help you stick to your promises to yourself. It may sound strange at first, but it has the amazing ability to make you much more likely to succeed at giving yourself at least one nourishing, re-energizing mini-sabbatical on the days when you need it the most.

Consider this: What if you put on your daily calendar in a visible notation from (let's say) 1:15pm until 1:35pm or from 2:00pm to 2:55pm a "Phantom Client" that looks on paper like a real appointment you cannot ignore, change or cancel? What's a Phantom Client? It's the name of someone who doesn't really exist but by putting this realistic name (how about the first name of your favorite grandparent) on your calendar you make it look (to your scanning brain) as if that spot is already taken and cannot be filled by anything else.

But instead of a meeting with your "Phantom Client," you can use that 15 or 30 or 55 minute time slot to take a brisk walk, to lock the door and meditate, to pray or read something spiritual and inspiring, or to do some stretching exercises or calm breathing. The name of the "Phantom Client" on your calendar says to your eyes and your brain, "This time slot is taken. It is reserved for someone you would not want to disappoint and you can't cancel a time slot that you've committed to be with this special person."

(If the word Phantom Client seems too playful or unprofessional to you, please feel free to change it to any crucial place-marker that works better for you. The trick is to make sure there is a 15 or 20 or 55 minute time slot that looks taken so that you can convince your own brain that this time slot can be used only for unwinding and taking a mini-sabbatical).

Here's how it works in real life on a very busy day:

The Man With the Calendar That Keeps Him on Track
Zach is an extremely busy and hard-working lawyer in a mid-sized firm who is also a devoted dad for his three kids. In recent years, Zach has rarely been able to keep his commitments to himself about unhooking from the pressure of "billable hours" and his worried doctor has told him that Zach is starting to get early-warning signs of two different serious ailments.

During one of our counseling sessions, Zach described to me how his good intentions to take a quick walk, meditate, or do some stretching exercises on a stressful day almost always get sidetracked by "another email, another phone call, or another document to review and correct." So I mentioned to him about the "Phantom Client" trick of reserving on your calendar (using the first name of your favorite grandparent) a few precious minutes for unwinding that I've seen work so successfully for many high-powered professionals.

Zach seemed slightly open to the idea for a few seconds and then his face tightened up with hesitation. I asked, "What was that thought?"

He replied, "It's my administrative assistant Bernice. She looks at my calendar all the time and she's going to be curious about who this 'Phantom Client' is that shows up a couple times a week on my calendar.

I asked Zach, "Does Bernice have a sense of humor and would it be possible for you to encourage her to have her own 'Phantom Client' (using her own favorite grandparent's first name) that she can schedule a couple times a week for a few minutes to help her unwind as well?"

Zach smiled and said, "Bernice does have a great sense of humor and she would be over the moon happy if I told her I was ok with the idea of her having a few fifteen or twenty minute mini-sabbaticals each week to keep her healthy and re-energized. We both know we are over-worked and close to our breaking points. If we can have this simple device be our little secret that we are both utilizing the 'Phantom Client' a few times a week, that would not only help us stay healthy and reduce sick days, but it would also strengthen the working relationship between us that has been a little frayed lately."

That was the beginning of a shift for Zach and also for his administrative assistant Bernice. They both began to use the "Phantom Client" as a way of guaranteeing that for at least 15 or 20 or 55 minutes every few days they each (at different times from one another) had a mini-sabbatical in which they could take a walk, stretch, close their eyes for a few minutes, or read something spiritual and uplifting to restore their energy on an over-filled week.

You might be asking: Why do human beings need a Phantom Client on our calendar in order to give ourselves the permission to follow through and unwind for 15 or 20 or 55 minutes a few times a week? I can't speak for you or anyone else. But I do know in my own life and for many of my counseling clients, there's something definitive about a name on the daily calendar that says, "This spot is taken." Then when you're in need of a 15 or 20 or 55 minute refresher, the time has already been reserved for you. The official-looking calendar slot makes it much easier to follow through on what nourishes your body, mind, and soul.

- Weekday Mini-Sabbatical Possibility #3: The "Plan B" Shavvat Va-yinafash for Jewish Leaders Who Are On Duty During the Weekly Shabbat

Now that we've been spending many pages together in this book, I need to share with you a deep dark secret about Jewish life in the 21st century. The deep dark secret is that most of the cherished role models in any temple or synagogue do not have the freedom to experience a relaxed Shabbat on Friday night or Saturday because in fact they are extremely busy at those times doing what others expect of them.

Think about it. If the rabbi, the cantor, the paid staff, the choir members, the synagogue board members, and the most active lay leadership are all handling lots of details, choreography, planning sessions, interrupted conversations, and time pressures to keep things moving smoothly at Friday night events and Saturday gatherings, then guess what—their sense of a restful and "no pressure" Shabbat didn't really happen yet for the week.

So when do the most active members and leaders of a congregation get to celebrate a day of rest or a chance to let go of all stress, pressure, and expectations? If they care about nourishing their own souls and being more fully alive, then they will need to carve out a mini-sabbatical of a few hours, a half day, or possibly an entire day on one of the other weekdays. It can have some similar "gift certificate" elements as the traditional Shabbat: a chance to walk and talk in a calmer way, a chance to enjoy a non-rushed meal with loved ones, an opportunity to feel relaxed and cuddly with a special someone, a unique time to be at one with the peacefulness of imagining a world where everyone has enough and doesn't need to work so hard all the time.

This joyful few hours or half-day or whole day might be hard to carve out at first. Clearly your schedule is already quite full or overfilled on most weeks. But if you get into the habit of looking for and reserving a block of time for your own mini-sabbatical and your quality time with loved ones, it will become much easier to make it happen on most weeks.   Here's a quick example of one Jewish leader who was Shabbat-deprived until she got creative and carved out a mini-sabbatical for her and her loved ones on a different day:

The Dedicated Woman Who Was Tired of Burning Out

Leah is a highly-respected Jewish educator who has always been someone that others look to for help, advice, and caring.   During her teens she took care of an ailing parent.   In college she took care of her emotionally-unstable boyfriend.   After college she began her teaching career and she also fell in love with a woman named Claire who was very charismatic and exciting, but who was away quite often on business trips.

Leah and Claire created a family together and are raising two young children, one of whom has special needs.   Much of the time, Leah is not only the parent who does most of the carpooling, meal-making, and late-night wake-ups, but Leah is also the hand-holder for several of the teachers on her staff at a very dynamic Jewish school.

When I first met Leah at a lecture I was giving, I was amazed at how many hats she wore extremely well—congregational board member, award-winning teacher, loyal daughter and older sister, devoted parent and committed partner.   Then a few months later, I received a phone call from Leah telling me, "I think I need to talk to someone.   I've got a recurring illness and my doc seems to believe that unless I learn to unhook from some of the pressures in my life I will just continue to have recurring bouts of being compromised by my over-taxed immune system."

That was the beginning of some excellent counseling sessions and a few carefully-considered shifts in her weekly schedule and way of living.   Leah still wears a number of the hats and roles that give her life joy and meaning.   But she's also become more mindful and strategic about how to carve out time each week for her own health, resilience, and re-energizing.

One of the most effective strategies that Leah now utilizes each week is to set aside a half day for experiencing what she describes as, "A mini-Shabbat that takes me out of the role of being on call for everyone who tugs at me and it frees me up to renew my sense of balance and well-being."

Specifically, Leah decided (like a Broadway theatre does) to take each Monday as her day off. She still teaches her students and supervises her staff on Saturday mornings and Sunday mornings. But on Mondays, she has gotten in the habit of "only doing things where I'm off the clock, out of the pressure-cooker. I set aside Mondays as my mini-Shabbat where I connect at lunch or dinner with friends and loved ones in a non-rushed way and I do the things that nourish my soul, such as reading uplifting books or taking a walk in nature with Claire (whenever she is in town) where we finally have time to reconnect and remember why we love each other so much."

According to Leah, "My first choice would be to celebrate Shabbat on Friday nights and on Saturday. But because I'm almost always on duty at those times doing things for the congregation and handling lots of requests and logistics, the only way for me to experience a day of gratefulness, healing, and peace is to set aside another day of the week for a 'Plan B' Shabbat. I love my work for the congregation and I love my students and staff. But there's something holy and beautiful about having several hours each Monday where I'm free to connect with my life and my family in a non-pressured way that truly makes me feel more alive."

As you think about your own weekly schedule, do you ever feel trapped or overloaded by all the time pressures and roles that you are handling? What if you were to set aside a half-day or a whole day on most weeks so that you were able to renew yourself and experience a profound "Shavvat va-yinafash," a chance to rest and restore your precious soul?   The feeling of being more fully alive will not only be satisfying on that one day set aside from the others, but your health and creativity will probably be much more vibrant for the rest of the week if you give yourself that gift certificate of "A Day to Respond to the Needs of Your Soul."

DISCUSSION QUESTIONS AND CONVERSATION STARTERS FROM THE BOOK "MORE FULLY ALIVE"

N ote: *These questions can be discussed in a study group, a class, a book group, a family conversation at the dinner table, a staff training workshop, on your own with a journal or note-pad, or in a one-on-one hevruta conversation between study partners or friends.*

Please respect and honor the unique viewpoints of each participant because these questions are not about "the right answer" but rather are meant to help each individual explore his or her own connection to Jewish ideas about health, resilience, creativity, balance, compassion, and holiness.

Chapter One: Reconnecting with the Nourishing Breath of Life
What are the moments recently when you felt constricted, pulled in two directions at once, anxious, tense, or "in mitzrayim" and it caused your breathing to be too narrow/shallow or too rapid/rushed?

What does it feel like when you test out the method described in Chapter One of saying silently, "Kol han-shamah, t'hallel Yah, every breath is celebrating the Source of Life," as you breathe in and out fully and calmly a few times?

What were you taught (or not taught) are the Jewish beliefs about God as the "breath of life" or as an ever-changing Creative Force that is beyond human definition?

When have you felt aligned and in synch with the Creative Flow and when have you felt cut off or out of synch with these subtle energies?

What is your personal belief about how your individual soul (your Neshamah) can connect more fully with the hard-to-describe Source of Life?

Chapter Two: Opening Your Heart Even When You're Feeling Impatient

What is a situation in your personal life, your work, or your family situation that tends to spark your impatience, irritation, or defensiveness, or when you start to notice your heart is not fully open?

What is your reaction to the phrases in Chapter Two about "circumcising your heart" or "opening up your heart" with a particular person who requires a lot from you or who sometimes gets on your nerves?

What did you experience when you did the exercise in Chapter Two in which you were in a tense conversation and you breathed calmly and fully while saying to yourself, "Is my heart open right now?"

What are your fears, concerns, or hesitations about being "too open" to someone who has hurt you in the past or who has been pushy or demanding at times?   Is it possible to listen with an open heart but not to get run over by this person?

When has your heart been somewhat closed to your own personal struggles and what would happen if you opened your heart a bit more regarding the challenging moments in your life?

Chapter Three: Finding a Healthy Balance in Situations That Could Rattle You

What is a situation in which you leaned too much in the direction of Chesed (lovingkindness, generosity, or flexibility) and it didn't turn out well?

What is a situation in which you leaned too much in the direction of Gevurah (rigidity, structure, or firmness) and it didn't turn out well?

What is a situation in your life right now where being "100% nice" or "100% strict" might not be appropriate, so instead what would be a healthy balance (a Tiferet possibility) for finding the right combination of kindness and structure?

Who in your life is the "much too nice" doormat person you don't want to emulate and who in your life is the "much too rigid" controlling person you don't want to emulate? Who is someone in your life who has shown you a few examples of what it means to be balanced and healthy between the extremes of "too nice" or "too rigid"—someone who can say "No" lovingly and who can balance the needs of others with one's own needs?

What are two examples from your own life when you felt sufficiently balanced (empathic-but-firm, loving-but-strong, structured-but-flexible), and how did you reach those balanced moments?

Chapter Four: Addressing the Fears and Pressures that Constrict You

What are a couple of fears you once had that you now have moved beyond for the most part?

What are the concerns and hesitations that currently interrupt your thoughts or hold you back from living more fully?

With regard to the phrase "All the world is just a narrow bridge and the main thing is not to fear," do you prefer the first interpretation from Chapter Four that says, "the main thing is not to fear at all," or do you prefer the second interpretation discussed in Chapter Four that says, "the main thing is not to be entirely in fear?"

When you think of a challenging situation in your life, what do you experience when you breathe calmly and fully in and out as you focus on the part of yourself that is "not completely afraid?"

What kind of internal and external support will you need in order to go forward successfully with something that currently feels anxiety-producing or complicated?

Chapter Five: Treating Your Body with Greater Understanding and Care

What do you envision when you say the words, "Refu-aht ha-nefesh, heal or renew my spirit?"

What do you envision when you say the words, "Refu-aht ha-guf, heal or renew my body?"

When you think about your own health challenges or the health challenges of someone you care about, what do you envision as "Refu-ah Sh'lay-ma, restoring this person to wholeness or completeness?"

In what ways have you taken your health or your body's fragile needs for granted, and what can you do to become a better steward or caretaker for this holy vessel that has been gifted to you?

What are the support systems you already have put together for healing or wholeness in your life (or in the life of someone you care about) and what are the supports you will need to add or improve?

Chapter Six: Exploring Inner Repair and Outer Repair

What is a personal character trait that you have been working on in the past and that still needs some additional layers of insight and improvement?

What is an aspect of repairing the world that touches you deeply and that you don't want to forget or ignore?

When you hear the phrase, "You are not obligated to complete the work, but neither are you free to abandon it," what comes to mind as a healthy way to stay involved in your personal growth or your repair of some aspect of the world without burning out?

Recall a time when you began to feel burned out or frustrated trying to change something in your personality traits or in the unfairness of the world around you…and it wasn't changing too quickly or too easily. Based on the approach in Chapter Six, what steps would help increase your resilience and your effectiveness in these slow-to-change situations?

What kind of teamwork, partnering, support, resources, creativity, or realistic time frames could help you be more effective and less frustrated in your quest to improve some aspect of yourself or the world around you?

Chapter Seven: Enjoying Mini-Sabbaticals Each Day and Each Week

What were you taught (or not taught) about the way to be on the Sabbath?

What do you currently enjoy about the Sabbath each week and what would you like to add or subtract from your practice of "Shavvat va-yinafash, restoring your soul" each week?

What are the moments in your weekdays when you could possibly take a five, ten, or fifty minute Mini-Sabbatical to renew your clarity, your creativity, or your sense of well-being?

What tends to block you or distract you from taking quiet moments each day or each week to listen to the deeper needs of your soul?

Recall a time in your life when you truly let go and connected with a non-pressured way of being, and what might be your next opportunity to experience this kind of nourishing at-one-ment again?

INFORMATION ABOUT
PRESENTATIONS BY THE AUTHOR

L eonard Felder, PhD works with temples, synagogues, non-prof-it groups, Hillel events, adult education programs, and book fairs to design workshops and presentations that help audiences combine Jewish spiritual wisdom and psychological wisdom to deal more effectively with stress, overload, complicated people, and tough decisions.

A few of the responses he has received in recent years include:

"Jewish Family Service had the pleasure last week of hearing Dr. Len Felder as the keynote speaker for an annual community lecture which drew more than 250 people. His warmth and ability to connect with people are remarkable. In addition to sharing his knowledge, he is funny and engaging throughout his presentation. His versatility in drawing from multiple sources, including his ability to weave in Jewish texts and thoughts in a seamless and non-denominational way, made his talks resonate with all types of individuals who told me that they were touched and inspired by his vivid stories and practical examples. I highly recommend Dr. Felder and look forward to hearing him again in the near future."

--Matt Greenberg, CEO, Jewish Family Service, Stamford, Connecticut

"That was one of the largest crowds we've ever had for a literary event. You were terrific not only with your depth and excellent teachings, but also with your humor and warmth. It's wonderful when someone so knowledgeable about Judaism is also so accessible and enjoyable to study with. We can't wait to have you back."
--Joyce Lit, Jewish Book Fair Director, Austin, Texas
"I knew you were a good writer but I didn't know what an amazing teacher and discussion leader you are. The entire congregation was so thankful that these holy teachings and important life issues could be explored in such a warm and lively way. Thank you for bringing your enthusiasm and your caring heart to us."
--Rabbi Marc Sirinsky, Temple Emek Shalom, Ashland, Oregon
"I have the definition of a successful program—that is when students and faculty are still talking about your program a week later. Several people have commented how fascinating it was, especially your amazing breadth of knowledge of multiple spiritual and psychological traditions. People loved your approach and I must concur it was a wonderful experience."
--Caty Konigsberg, Hillel Director, Occidental College, California

If you would like to discuss possible times and topics for a presentation by Len Felder, PhD, you can contact him directly at 310 815-1611 or LCFelder@yahoo.com

ACKNOWLEDGEMENTS

This book has been stirring inside me for many years and I am grateful to all the individuals who helped me sort out the questions and choices that led to these seven chapters.

Many teachers, rabbis, and study partners have been generous and kind as we explored these topics. It started at Temple Israel in Detroit when I was growing up and I was guided by Rabbi M. Robert Syme, Helen Gilbert, Cantor Harold Orbach, and my study partners and lifelong friends Nancy Shapiro Pikelny, Michael Resnick, Catherine Mahlin, Barbara Schlain Polsky, and Gayle Belin. When I lived in New York and San Diego, I studied with many wise teachers and friends, including Sonny Stokes, Bob Mandel, Mallie Burzon, Sondra Ray, Linda Thistle, Binnie Dansby, Doretta Winkelman, Wendy Piuck, Adelaide Bry, Dr. Harold Bloomfield, Sirah Vettese, Dr. Viktor Frankl, and Dr. Elisabeth Kubler-Ross.

Since moving to Los Angeles I have enjoyed learning from many friends and teachers, including Teri Bernstein, Peter Reiss, Carol Reiss, Trudi Alexy Sternlicht, Dr. Miriam Raviv, Dr. Sandra Kaler, Lucky Altman, Glen Poling, Neil Van Steenbergen, Janet Sternfeld Davis, Howard Davis, Dr. Melinda Garcia, Glen Effertz, Catherine Coulson, Rabbi Marc Sirinsky, Rabbi Ted Falcon, Rabbi Alfred Wolf, Rabbi Laura Geller, Rabbi Sue Levi Elwell, Rabbi Zalman Schachter-Shalomi, Rabbi David Wolfe-Blank, Rabbi Mordecai

Finley, Rabbi David Cooper, Rabbi Stan Levy, Rabbi Deborah Orenstein, Rabbi Anne Brener, Rabbi Jackie Redner, Rabbi Diane Eliot, Rabbi Susan Nanus, Rabbinic Intern Greg Metzger, Rabbinic Intern Florence Dann, Jean Katz, Dr. Julie Madorsky, Dr. Vivian Gold, Dr. Phil Danufsky, Coleman Colla, Nadine Antin Colla, Rita Reuben, Marion Klein, Pattye Asarch, Kimball Marsh, Helene Silber, Judith Weinberger, and Judy Weintraub.   A special thank you goes to Rabbi Miriam Hamrell, who has been my rabbi, Musar teacher, and friend for the past 12 years.

I want to thank each of my counseling clients who have explored spiritual growth issues with me in private.   I am especially grateful to be learning every day from my wise and honest wife and best friend Linda Schorin and our beautiful and caring son Steven, and from my family in Michigan, Florida and New York, including Martin and Ena Felder, Helen Rothenberg Felder, Janice and Craig Ruff, Andi Bittker, Ruthe Wagner, Erica Ruff, and Ben Guralnik.   I also want to thank all of the members of the Schorin and Wilstein families who have been so loving and supportive over the years.

Most of all, I felt guided in the research and writing of this book by an Infinite Creative Source that is beyond description and words.   I am extremely thankful for all that has been given to me and for all that I have been able to share with others.

ABOUT THE AUTHOR

Leonard Felder, Ph.D. is a licensed psychologist in West Los Angeles whose books on personal growth and Jewish spirituality have sold over 1 million copies and were translated into 15 languages. His titles include *The Ten Challenges, Here I Am, Seven Prayers that Can Change Your Life, Fitting In Is Overrated, When Difficult Relatives Happen to Good People, Wake Up or Break Up, When a Loved One is Ill,* and *Making Peace with Your Parents.*

He has appeared on over 150 radio and television interview programs, including *National Public Radio, Pacifica Radio, The Today Show on NBC, Oprah Winfrey, CNN, ABC News, Canada AM, BBC London, and ABC Australia.* He has also been invited to speak at more than 50 synagogues and temples nationwide, as well as 20 Jewish book fairs.

Some of the awards Dr. Felder has received are the Nonfiction Book of the Year 1985 from *Medical Self-Care Magazine,* Best Jewish Writing 2002 from Jossey-Bass Annual Review, Nonfiction Book of the Year 2008 from *Body and Soul Magazine,* Runner Up for Best Spiritual Writing 2008 from the Books for a Better Life Foundation, and the Distinguished Merit Citation of the National Conference of Christians and Jews 1987 for developing programs to combat racism, sexism, homophobia, and religious prejudice.

Originally from Detroit, Michigan, he attended Kenyon College in Ohio and was the Director of Research for Doubleday and Company in New York before becoming a psychologist. Dr. Felder and his wife Linda Schorin live in Mar Vista, California and they are the parents of a young adult who has special needs.

For more information about Dr. Felder and his writings and talks, please visit www.morefullyalive.net

www.ingramcontent.com/pod-product-compliance
Lightning Source LLC
LaVergne TN
LVHW011351080426
835511LV00005B/235